ON THE TRAIL OF
AN UNCERTAIN DREAM

IMMIGRANT COMMUNITIES & ETHNIC MINORITIES IN THE UNITED STATES & CANADA: No. 38

ISSN 0749-5951

Series Editor: Robert J. Theodoratus
Department of Anthropology, Colorado State University

1. James G. Chadney. *The Sikhs of Vancouver.*
2. Paul Driben. *We Are Metis: The Ethnography of a Halfbreed Community in Northern Alberta.*
3. A. Michael Colfer. *Morality, Kindred, and Ethnic Boundary: A Study of the Oregon Old Believers.*
4. Nanciellen Davis. *Ethnicity and Ethnic Group Persistence in an Acadian Village in Maritime Canada.*
5. Juli Ellen Skansie. *Death Is for All: Death and Death-Related Beliefs of Rural Spanish-Americans.*
6. Robert Mark Kamen. *Growing Up Hasidic: Education and Socialization in the Bobover Hasidic Community.*
7. Liucija Baskauskas. *An Urban Enclave: Lithuanian Refugees in Los Angeles.*
8. Manuel Alers-Montalvo. *The Puerto Rican Migrants of New York City.*
9. Wayne Wheeler. *An Analysis of Social Change in a Swedish-Immigrant Community: The Case of Lindsborg, Kansas.*
10. Edwin B. Almirol. *Ethnic Identity and Social Negotiation: A Study of a Filipino Community in California.*
11. Stanford Neil Gerber. *Russkoya Celo: The Ethnography of a Russian-American Community.*
12. Peter Paul Jonitis. *The Acculturation of the Lithuanians of Chester, Pennsylvania.*
13. Irene Isabel Blea. *Bessemer: A Sociological Perspective of a Chicano Bario.*
14. Dorothy Ann Gilbert. *Recent Portuguese Immigrants to Fall River, Massachusetts: An Analysis of Relative Economic Success.*
15. Jeffrey Lynn Eighmy. *Mennonite Architecture: Diachronic Evidence for Rapid Diffusion in Rural Communities.*
16. Elizabeth Kathleen Briody. *Household Labor Patterns among Mexican Americans in South Texas: Buscando Trabajo Seguro.*
17. Karen L. S. Muir. *The Strongest Part of the Family: A Study of Lao Refugee Women in Columbus, Ohio.*
18. Judith A. Nagate. *Continuity and Change Among the Old Order Amish of Illinois.*
19. Mary G. Harris. *Cholas: Latino Girls and Gangs.*
20. Rebecca B. Aiken. *Montreal Chinese Property Ownership and Occupational Change, 1881–1981.*
21. Peter Vasiliadis. *Dangerous Truths: Interethnic Competition in a Northeastern Ontario Goldmining Community.*
22. Bruce La Brack. *The Sikhs of Northern California, 1904–1975: A Socio—Historical Study.*
23. Jenny K. Phillips. *Symbol, Myth, and Rhetoric: The Politics of Culture in an Armenian-American Population.*
24. Stacy G. H. Yap. *Gather Your Strength, Sisters: The Emerging Role of Chinese Women Community Workers.*
25. Phyllis Cancilla Martinelli. *Ethnicity In The Sunbelt: Italian-American Migrants in Scottsdale, Arizona.*
26. Dennis L. Nagi. *The Albanian-American Odyssey: A Pilot Study of the Albanian Community of Boston, Massachusetts.*
27. Shirley Ewart. *Cornish Mining Families of Grass Valley, California.*
28. Marilyn Preheim Rose. *On the Move: A Study of Migration and Ethnic Persistence among Mennonites from East Freeman, South Dakota.*
29. Richard H. Thompson. *Toronto's Chinatown: The Changing Social Organization of an Ethnic Community.*
30. Bernard Wong. *Patronage, Brokerage, Entrepreneurship and the Chinese Community of New York.*

Continued at back of book

ON THE TRAIL OF AN UNCERTAIN DREAM
Indian Immigrant Experience in America

Sathi S. Dasgupta

AMS Press, Inc.
New York

Library of Congress Cataloging-in-Publication Data

Dasgupta, Sathi Sengupta.
  On the trail of an uncertain dream.
  p. cm. — (Immigrant communities & ethnic minorities in the United States & Canada ; 38)
  Bibliography: p.
  Includes index.
  ISBN 0-404-19448-6
  1. East Indian Americans. 2. Immigrants—United States. 3. United States—Emigration and immigration. 4. India—Emigration and immigration. I. Title. II. Series.
  E184.E2D37 1989
  305.8'91411'073   88-46198

All AMS books are printed on acid-free paper that meets the guidelines for performance and durability of the Committee on Production Guidelines for Book Longevity of the Council on Library Resources.

Copyright © 1989 by AMS PRESS, INC.
All rights reserved.

AMS PRESS, INC.
56 East 13th Street
New York, N.Y. 10003, U.S.A.

MANUFACTURED IN THE UNITED STATES OF AMERICA

To Mona and Sumit
The First Generation

TABLE OF CONTENTS

		Page
PREFACE		ix
I	INTRODUCTION	1
II	THEORETICAL FRAMEWORK	6
III	DATA COLLECTION	22
IV	BECOMING AN IMMIGRANT	39
V	CULTURAL SELECTIVITY AS CULTURAL SURVIVAL	65
VI	THE DYNAMICS OF CONJUGAL RELATIONS	92
VII	THE DYNAMICS OF PARENT CHILD RELATIONS	118
VIII	THE INDIAN IMMIGRANT WOMEN	131
IX	THE WORLD OF OCCUPATION	161
X	SUMMARY AND CONCLUSION	188
APPENDIX		200
BIBLIOGRAPHY		205
NOTES		200
INDEX		215

PREFACE

The idea of writing a book on Indian immigrants evolved out of my personal experience of living in the American society as an immigrant. Immigrants in America face considerable hardship, frustration, isolation and alienation as they try to find a niche in the American society. I was not an exception. Additionally, I experienced a sense of confusion since I felt that I had no right to experience these negative emotions since I came to America voluntarily and was free to go back any time I wanted to. It was this sense of confusion and ambivalence that inspired me to select Indian immigrants as my subjects of research. I agree with C.W. Mills that all our personal experience has public roots. Through my research, I wanted to build that bridge between my personal experience as an immigrant and the sociological fact of being an immigrant from India in the American society.

I have tried to describe the experience and way of life of Indian immigrants as they might describe it themselves as if they are sociologists. My interviewees have done an excellent job, no less than if it would have been done by trained sociologists. My only hope is that I have done as good a job of portraying their experiences in the American society, as they have done relating it.

I hoped to achieve another objective through this study. The majority of immigrants from India came during the mid-sixties to fulfill the need for technical and professional labor in the American society. Apart from their existence as workers, Indian immigrants have remained secluded, unheeded, and unobtrusive in the American society. Text books on Racial and Ethnic minorities ignore them. Nobody even has bothered to make them the butt of ethnic jokes. I hope my research will validate their existence as viable subjects of social science research.

There were numerous individuals who helped to put together this work. My teachers and advisors, Maggie Andersen, Jerry Turkel and Sally Bould were very patient in reading the manuscript over and over again and offering valuable comments and suggestions. I am extremely grateful to them for their support throughout my research. I also thank my friends and cohorts Margie Starrels and Dave Costello for their help in editing the manuscript. I am also thankful to editor Dr. Robert Theodoratus for taking an interest in my study and selecting it for publication.

Finally, I would like to thank my family members for putting up with me during the time I was doing my research

PREFACE

and writing the manuscript. I especially thank my children Mona and Sumit for being so considerate and understanding when mom could not be there to take care of them.

CHAPTER ONE

INTRODUCTION

The present study analyzes the process of becoming an 'immigrant' for Indians in the U.S. and the methods these immigrants use to develop and define a web of social relationships in their adopted country.

The present research studies the Indian immigrants as an emerging ethnic group and the boundaries they set which define their identities and differentiate them from the 'others' in the American society on the basis of selective cultural attributes. The study also analyzes the mechanisms used by the Indian immigrants to ensure their viable survival as an ethnic group in American society.

The Indian immigrants in the United States constitute a selective group due to the nature of the 1965 Immigration Act. This Act opened up a floodgate of immigration from the Eastern hemisphere countries. The McCarren-Walter Act of 1952 had reaffirmed the previously existing national origin quota system. Although the Act supposedly removed race as a barrier to immigration, for the orientals slots were still assigned on the basis of race rather than place of birth.

A British born Indian, for example had to apply for entry on the Indian quota, whereas other native born Britishers could enter on a non quota basis as natives of a western hemisphere country.

The 1965 Immigration Act phased out the national origin quota system and eventually all visas became available on a first come first serve basis. The Act, however, incorporated a preference system for the Eastern hemisphere countries. Thus, preferential entry status was given to visa applicants who were either relatives of U.S. citizens or workers with skills which were needed in the U.S. The new law also distinguished among skill levels and gave higher preference to persons with professional qualifications or with relatives who would employ them. The 1965 Act also made changes in the labor certification procedures. The Act specified that individuals from Eastern hemisphere countries could not enter the U.S. as workers unless the Secretary of Labor certified that there was a shortage of qualified workers in their particular professional field and that alien workers' presence would not adversely affect wages and working conditions of the native born workers.

The 1965 Immigration Act thus encouraged the entry of professional workers in the U.S. Since professional education in India is patterned after the British and

American educational system, and the instruction is in English, the 1965 Act caused an influx of professional workers from India who were also proficient in both spoken and written English. The Indian immigrants also came during a period when there was a demand for highly skilled workers in the fields of science and technology. The Indian immigrants' occupations in high demand fields have been very relevant to their adjustment within the American society.

The fact that these educated immigrants came mainly from the urban centers of India also made them somewhat different from earlier immigrants who came from the rural areas of European societies. The Indian immigrants, due to their technical and professional background and their proficiency in the English language, found it easier to get jobs in the professional fields shortly after they immigrated to the U.S. Thus, unlike the other immigrant groups, they did not have to undergo Americanization training in order to gain access to the amenities associated with middle class life styles. Stephen Steinberg (1981: 256) notes that when ethnicity is associated with class disadvantages, poverty, hardship and a low standard of living, a powerful inducement exists for that group to assimilate into the mainstream, since this will improve their chances for a better life. Since the Indian immigrants have found their life conditions in the American society better than they had expected, the pressure for assimilation is not felt that intensely. Middle class life style is not seen as dependent upon assimilation into the mainstream life. On the other hand, their class position has enabled them to maintain their cultural identity.

Because of these differences between the Indian immigrants and other ethnic groups, the pre-existing theories of assimilation which were mainly based on the experiences of the European immigrants, are severely inadequate to analyze the experiences of the Indian immigrants. Existing theories of assimilation overemphasize the idea of eventual assimilation of the immigrants in to the mainstream American life. Even the cultural pluralist theories of Glazer and Moynihan are preoccupied with the idea of "assimilation and absorption to a homogeneous mass." (1963: 70) The theories are deterministic in the sense that immigrants are seen as passive individuals who were either rapidly or slowly assimilating. The sociologists studying the early ethnic groups, looked at the disorganization emanating from the lack of fit between the previously existing norms and the new social system while ignoring the emergence of a new social structure or a gradually emerging fabric of social relationships.

The present study, thus, instead of analyzing how the Indian immigrants measure in terms of their eventual assimilation, will emphasize how the Indian immigrants are developing a nexus of social relationships to define their ethnicity.

Chapter two deals with clarifying the theoretical concepts that form the groundwork for analyzing the ethnicity of the Indian immigrants in the U.S. Chapter Three describes the methods of collecting data. Chapter Four analyzes the process of becoming an immigrant on the part of the Indians in the U.S. Chapter Five discusses the dilemmas in value orientations experienced by the Indian immigrants in the U.S. Chapters Six and Seven examine the conjugal relationships and parent child relationships within an Indian immigrant family. Since ethnicity is related to the gender divisions existing in a particular society, Chapter Eight deals with the positions of the Indian woman in the American society. Chapter Nine analyzes the world of work and occupation of the Indian immigrants. Chapter Ten tries to put the ethnicity of the Indian immigrants within the broader social matrix of the American society.

CHAPTER TWO

THEORETICAL FRAMEWORK

Assimilation has been defined as a "process by which persons who are unlike in their social heritage come to share the same body of sentiments, traditions and loyalties (Reuter: 1941: 84). Park defines assimilation

> as a process interpenetration and fusion in which persons and groups acquire the memories, sentiments and attitudes of other persons or groups and, by shaping their experience and history are incorporated with them in a common cultural life.

The dominant theme that runs through these definitions of assimilation is that persons "embrace" and "share" the existing body of culture. Mitchell (1968) in The Dictionary of Sociology states that assimilation is the substitution of one nationality pattern for another. Ordinarily, the modifications must be made by the weaker or numerically inferior group (pp. 276-77). Hence, assimilation is seen as a process by which the assimilating group is seen as taking up the culture of the dominant group of the society.

According to the Anglo-conformity theory, the dominant group is presumed to be Anglo-Saxon Protestant. The basic

THEORETICAL FRAMEWORK

contention is that, over time, all groups will conform to the mores of life, lifestyles and values of the dominant majority. One of the prominent proponents of the Anglo-conformity theory is S. N. Eisenstadt. According to him, the process of absorption, from the immigrants' point of view may be seen as one of "institutionalizing" their role expectations. The institutionalization involves several closely connected processes. First, they have to acquire new skills and learn to make use of various new mechanisms like language, technical orientations, ecological orientations and so on. Second, they have to learn how to perform various new roles necessary in the new society. Third, they have gradually had to rebuild and reform their ideal of themselves and their status images by acquiring new sets of values. Eisenstadt says that the process of absorption is synonymous to the process of "resocialization". (1954: 10) To summarize, the process of absorption, according to Eisenstadt, from the point of view of the immigrants, entails the learning of new roles, the transformation of primary group values, and the extension of participation beyond the primary group in the main spheres of the social system.

The Anglo-conformity theory of assimilation, however, sees assimilation as a one sided process whereby the immigrant groups assume the culture of the dominant group.

The Amalgamation theory, on the other hand, maintains that different groups over time become a new group which is different from the original group but is a combination of them all. Fichter says that amalgamation is a process whereby groups accept and perform one another's patterns of behavior. Fichter, however, says that the process is not one sided, but "it is a relation of interaction in which both parties behave reciprocally even though one may be much more affected than the other." (1957: 229) Assimilation, according to this definition signifies a reciprocal exchange where different patterns of behavior interact in such a way that a common culture is developed.

Newman (1973: 55), however, has pointed out that for amalgamation to occur, the majority group must allow and encourage the minority groups to assimilate and amalgamate and that minority groups will assimilate and amalgamate either voluntarily or involuntarily. While both these conditions might prevail in some situations, this is rarely the case. Moreover, for amalgamation to occur, the majority group must relinquish some of their culture and position of dominance in the society. Few dominant groups in the history of mankind have voluntarily relinquished their power and position.

Both the Anglo-conformity and Amalgamation theories view assimilation as a uni-dimensional linear process whereby the ethnic groups eventually assimilate in the American society. The theories are extremely deterministic in viewing the assimilation process as free from individual discretion. The theories portray the immigrants as passive subjects waiting to be assimilated in the American society.

The Cultural pluralists like Kallan (1924) and Novak (1972), on the other hand, view ethnic groups as maintaining their own unique identities. Kallan (1924) sees the members of the ethnic groups as consciously identifying with the traits of the group to which their ancestors belong. These traits form the "identity kit" for the members of the groups. Novak (1972) notes the persistence of ethnicity in the social, cultural, and religious practices of America's white ethnics. He is eloquent in his support of the continuities of new ethnic awareness and calls for a recognition of the legitimate expressions of self-identity on the part of the American ethnic community. Novak reiterates that "people uncertain of their own idenity are not wholly free." (1972: 3)

Novak (1972) sees the ethnic communities as offering a "gemeinschaft" world to its members. The same thing is being seen by Jean Martin (1981) who sees the ethnic communities as sources of ascribed relations. She writes that the importance of ethnic communities lies in the fact that

> our society is patently overburdened with situations in which what we are has to be repeatedly achieved, demonstrated and proved while it is just as short of communal ties based on ascriptions. (1981: 122)

The cultural pluralists, however, see the immigrants as passive people living in a pluralistic society and belonging to ethnic communities which are uniform in structure. They do not take into account the internal differentiations characterizing different ethnic groups. Besides the immigrants are rarely seen by the cultural pluralists as members of an emerging social structure with a life of its own. The emphasis of the cultural pluralists lies on "primordial cultures" or in examining the items of past cultures preserved rather than on the web of social relationships or new cultural packages developed by the immigrants as result of their living experiences in a foreign society.

Glazer and Moynihan (1963) in an effort to enrich the existing theories of assimilation define assimilation as a group process, a process leading to the formation of new social form as a result of assimilation. They, for the first time, see the immigrants as belonging to an ethnic group and not isolated individuals who are at different stages of assimilation. They (1963) observe that as far as immigrants are concerned, both assimilation and cultural pluralism have occurred in the American society. "As the

THEORETICAL FRAMEWORK

groups were transformed by influences in the American society, stripped of their original attributes, they were recreated as something new but still as identifiable groups. The assimilating power of the American society and culture operated on immigrant groups in different ways to make them, it is true, something they had not been, but still something distinct and identifiable." (13-14) The impact of assimilation on the groups is different because the groups are different and also because American society does not assimilate immigrants fully or in equal degrees (p. 14).

The distinctiveness of the groups is maintained by two ways: firstly by "family and fellow feeling" which "bind the ethnic group" ... The ethnic group is something of an extended family or tribe which provides comfort and material support (p. 18). Second, the ethnic groups such as those in New York city are also interest groups. Each group in turn becomes politically organized in order to fight for its rights and privileges.

However, Glazer and Moynihan see the ethnic groups as being recreated by the American society and not as something which emerges as a crystallization of social relationships developed by the members themselves. They also do not see the ethnic groups as structures in relation to the larger social matrix in which they are anchored.

Ethnicity should not be viewed as a primordial "given"

but as a phenomenon which can be managed, negotiated, aligned or manipulated somehow for a variety of expressive or instrumental reasons by the members themselves. Ethnic group formation may be seen in political, economic and cultural terms. Seen in political and economic terms, ethnic group formation may represent utilization of political and economic resources. But ethnic manifestation may also be primarily cultural in nature (Deshen, 1975: 282). Such a manifestation might be interpreted primarily as "strategies" to solve the problem of identity, belief and culture and perhaps secondarily as political strategies.

A cultural ethnic group, on the other hand, shares a common set of values, experiences, behavioral characteristics and linguistic traits which differ significantly from those of other ethnic groups within the society. Members of cultural ethnic groups pass on the symbols, language and other components of the cultural heritage to the next generations. The individual's ethnic cultural heritage is a source of pride and group identification (Bank and Gay, 1978: 245). A cultural ethnic group provides a network of personal relations which are based on ascription and not on achievement. "It provides a network of preferred individual and institutional affiliations through which primary group relations are established" (Bank and Gay, 1978: 245). Moreover, it

THEORETICAL FRAMEWORK

provides a "cultural screen" (Gordon, 1964) through which patterns of behavior and value systems of other ethnic groups are defined and assigned meaning.

Bank and Gay conclude that ethnicity is situational. (1978:251). They see ethnicity mostly in terms of satisfying the identity needs of the ethnic members. They say that the nature of identity need determines the "ethnic posture" of the groups at any time. That need may be expressed in the forms of reaffirmation of cultural identity or the recollection and reaffirmation of historical experiences, the manipulation of social forces to benefit ethnic group members, or the gaining of political and economic power to advance the group's social position. These needs determine whether the ethnic groups function as an economic, political or cultural group.

The identity needs of an ethnic group, however, should be seen in relation to the larger social matrix in which they are experienced. Mitchell says

> the perception of ethnic understanding becomes an understanding which has meaning for the social action of the people concerned, but this meaning is clearly contained within the social situation in which the interaction is taking place. (1974: 21)

In this connection, it is important to distinguish between "social setting" and "social situation" (Mitchell, 1978: 24). Setting refers to the macroscopic political, administrative and economic structures in which migration takes place, the overall structure of ethnic groups relations in a given society, the relative political, socio-economic status of these groups and the distribution of occupation, education, income, wealth and other social and material resources among them. Situation, on the other hand, refers to the more microscopic particular set of circumstances in which a migrants finds themselves. The emphasis is on the way in which individuals appraise the behavorial choices open to them, given the constraints imposed upon them by the wider setting. Thus the structural features of the setting provide the overall framework of social relations while at the level of situation, the concern is on the different courses of action actors may then pursue according to their understanding of their personal circumstances within this framework. Ethnicity, thus can be viewed in its cognitive and structural aspects. The cognitive aspect refers to the perception of the situation by the immigrants themselves and subsequent courses of social action taken by them. The structural aspect, on the other hand, refers to the wider macroscopic structure within which such perceptions are experienced.

Barth (1969) is one of the foremost social anthropologists associated with a cognitive aspect of ethnicity. He conceptualizes the ethnic groups as categories of ascription or identification by the actors

THEORETICAL FRAMEWORK   Page 15

themselves and also by others. Barth says that the process of formation of an ethnic group is a process of ascription and identification by the actors. The actors draw the boundaries around themselves to dichotomize between the insiders and the outsiders based on the cultural features they consider significant (1969: 10). Barth, furthermore, says that although ethnic categories sometimes coincide with cultural differences, most of the time they do not. Features that are taken into account by the ethnic groups are not the sum total of objective differences but only those which the actors regard as significant. He contends that some features are used by the actors as signals and emblems of differences themselves and while other features are ignored. Barth maintains that the continuity of an ethnic group depends on the maintenance of boundaries whereby the group maintains its own identity when its members interact with the non-members and dichotomize between the 'insiders' and the 'outsiders.' There are certain value orientations and standards of excellence which are made organizationally relevant by the ethnic groups and are emphasized to define the boundaries around the group. Barth says "ethnic categories provide an organizational vessel that may be given varying amounts of forms of content in different socio-cultural systems." (1969: 14)

Barth (1969) views the significance of ethnicity as

essentially "dependent on the actors' perceptions and understandings of the ethnic diacritica." (Okamura, 1978: 450) He attributes to ethnicity an existence of its own independent of the social context. Thus his exclusive emphasis on the cognitive aspect of ethnicity has been criticized as reducing ethnicity to subjective factors of identity. According to Okamura, the difficulty with this reasoning is that

> It would appear to accord to individuals the options to pursue whatever course of action they desire without consideration of the role constraints that may well proscribe such behavior. On the other hand, the structural setting may allow for variance of assertions of ethnicity. (1981: 458)

The structural dimension of ethnicity refers to the constraints imposed upon the actors in social situations as a result of overall structure of ethnic group relations in a society. Thus Epstein (1978: XVI) says that for the individual, acquisition of an ethnic identity always involves some element of choice. But such a choice is subject to a number of social constraints which relate to certain features of the social system. Steinberg (1981: IX) states that ethnic patterns should always be related to the larger social matrix in which they are embedded. He says that ethnicity involves ways of things, feelings and acting which constitute the essence of culture. But culture is integrally a part of the larger social process.

THEORETICAL FRAMEWORK

Steinberg sees cultural factors as conditioned by class factors. While accounting for the relative success of the Asians and Jews, Steinberg says that to whatever extent a reverence for learning was part of the religious and cultural heritage of the Asians and Jews, "it was activated and given existential significance by their social class circumstances." (1981: 132) These cultural factors interacting with class factors are influential in explaining Jewish success. He furthermore writes that " cultural values assume, operational significance in their interaction with a wider set of structural factors", (1981: 138) especially the advantageous position occupied by the economically mobile Jews and the favorable structure of educational opportunity that they encountered. Steinberg concludes that without the favorable social class circumstances, these groups would not have been able to maintain their traditional value of education. Thus, cultural factors need favorable circumstances to thrive and work for the ethnic group.

Gordon sees ethnic groups as "eth-class" or as subsocieties "created by the intersection of the vertical stratification of ethnicity with the horizontal stratification of social class." (19674: 52) Gordon says that with regard to cultural behavior, differences of social class are more important than differences in ethnic groups.

Thus, people of the same class tend to act alike even if they belong to different ethnic groups. People, however, tend to confine social participation in primary groups and primary relationships to their own social class segment within their own ethnic group. Thus, with a person of the same social class but of a different ethnic group, one shares behavorial similarities but not a sense of peoplehood. With those of the same ethnic group, but of a different social class, one shares a sense of peoplehood but not behavioral similarities. The only group which meets both these criteria are people of the same ethnic group and same social class.

Current research on ethnicity suggests that assimilation is not the inevitable outcome of the attainment of middle class status (Ryan, 1974; Novak, 1971; Rose, 1972). Thus Dillingham points out that to the extent that improved socio-economic status may provide middle class Blacks with the economic benefits of the class position but not the assurances of social equality, ethnicity will remain an important basis of identification (1976: 446).

In this connection, it is worthwhile to distinguish between the concepts of "class status" and "social status". Weber says that class status can be measured in terms of control or lack of it over goods and services as well as possible exploitation of these goods and services for the attainment of income or receipts within a given economic order. Social status, on the other hand, is based on claims to positive or negative privileges with respect to social prestige so far as it rests on one or more of the following bases: (a) development of a peculiar style of life; (b) hereditary charisma based on prestige of birth; (c) appropriation of political or hierocratic authority as a monopoly by socially distinct groups. (1947: 424) Weber says that social status may be based on class status but it is not determined by this alone. Property or managerial positions are not always sufficient to lend their holders a certain social status if these individuals lack the prestige of birth or position of political authority (1947: 428).

Thus, class status may provide an ethnic group or its members economic benefits but not social status or the assurance of social equality. Dillingham writes that based on the extent that the members of an ethnic group experience "status inconsistency as a result of which they are denied social equality and thus are structurally isolated," (1976: 446) ethnicity will remain an important basis of identification. Thus, to the extent that upward mobility provides an ethnic group "class status" and not "social status", it will be accompanied by stronger group identification and a resurgence of ethnic consciousness.

Ethnicity, thus should be seen in the context of the

social structure in which it is anchored. The larger social setting refers to the macroscopic political, administrative and economic circumstances in which migration takes place, the relative political and socio-economic status of these groups, and the distribution of occupation, education, income, wealth and other social and material resources among them. These macroscopic factors provide the context within which the identity choices of the ethnic group members are determined. The identity choice of the ethnic group members determines the "ethnic posture" of the ethnic group members. It determines the nature of significant relationships developed by the ethnic group members. Ethnicity, thus should be seen in terms of a dialectical inter-relationship between the cognitive aspects of ethnic identity and the structure of the society within which it is circumscribed.

The ethnic identity of an individual; may be predominantly cultural, political or economic. In cases, where the ethnicity takes the form of cultural reaffirmation of one's identity, the cultural features taken into account by the ethnic group members to define their identity are conditioned by their class position within the society. The class factor, however, should distinguish between "class status" and "social status". The former refers to a concept defined in economic terms and is measured mostly in terms of possession of material goods and services, and the latter refers to a concept measured mostly in terms of social prestige accorded to the individuals.

CHAPTER THREE
DATA COLLECTION

This stydy analyzes the cognitive and structural aspects of the ethnicity of Indian immigrants. The cognitive aspect of ethnicity involves how the immigrants appraise the behavorial choices open to them, given the constraints imposed upon them by the social structure. The structural aspect of ethnicity includes a consideration of the ethnic groups as units existing in relation to the social situation in which they exist. Since the cognitive perspective of ethnicity emphasizes the immigrant's understanding of their behavioral choices in concrete circumstances, a symbolic interactionist approach geared toward exploring subjects' definitions of the social situation follows. This approach warrants that:

> a research scholar who is concerned with the social actions of a given individual or a group ... or with a given type of social action, must see the action from the position of whoever is forming the action.... This means seeing the situation as it is seen by the actor, observing what the actor takes into account, observing how he interprets what is taken into account, noting the alternative kinds of acts that are mapped out in advance and seeking to follow the interpretation that led to the selection and

DATA COLLECTION   Page 23

      execution of one of these prefigured acts
      (Blumer 1969: 56).

Thus, in a symbolic interactionist approach, the concepts develop out of the data rather than regulate it.

SELECTION OF AN INDIAN COMMUNITY AND GAINING ENTRY

From the beginning of the research, it was known that there are several pockets on the east coast where a congregation of Indians could be found. There were, however, several restrictions. First, because of the limited financial resources, research had to be restricted to a local area within commuting distance. Second, India is a country of fourteen different languages. The researcher cannot speak any Indian languages other than her regional language. Because of the paucity of resources to hire an interpreter, interviews had to be conducted with people who could speak the language of the researcher. The interviews were not conducted in English because the interviewees can speak and understand English in varying degrees. Since the interviews were meant to be in-depth, whereby the interviewees would bring out infomation on their own, it was thought that communication in their native language would be most effective. The intention was to communicate with the interviewees freely and to let the interviewees express themselves most effectively. It was thought that these two purposes could be served only if communication with the interviewees was made through the native language of the researcher. Thus, an area had to be selected which was within the commuting distance and was inhabited by Indians who could speak Bengali, the native language of the researcher. Fortunately, an area was found which met all the specific requirements.

Confinement of the sample to one linguistic group was not thought to be significant enough to limit the generalizability of the research to the Indian community as a whole. The researcher's own communications and experience with members of different linguistic groups suggested that language is not a very significant factor in distinguishing the social and emotional experiences of different Indian immigrants.

Another researcher of the Indian scene, Hedwig Bachamann claimed that all over India, the Indians have very much the same moral code and outlook on life, inspite of regional, linguistic and caste differences. She writes:

> The many different peoples of India possess a fundamental common ethical trait which is prescribed by the moral doctrines and laws of its ancient sages, was stamped upon even the humble classes of the people. Hence a peculiar popular unity is imparted to the whole folk, based on nothing but the heritage bequeathed by the moral teachers and philosophers (1942: 14).

Aileen Ross, who wrote an insightful book on the Hindu

DATA COLLECTION

family in an urban setting, also centered her research in Bangalore, an important city in South India. Although her sample came from the local areas, she generalized her findings to the Indian society as a whole, claiming that "although details of life and custom vary markedly in different parts of India, the Hindu family everywhere has a basic structure which permits generalizations." (1961:15) Ross's findings will be cited in the course of this study to understand the Indian society, its values and its family structures.

After the area was selected, the next problem was gaining entry. The researcher had one advantage and that was her familiarity with the area and superficial knowledge of the Bengali community living there. The researcher had attended a few of their cultural festivals and shows they hold every year. The researcher also knew one or two families through mutual friends.

The first one or two interviews had to be done very carefully. One had to be very cautious not to ask any sensitive questions about interviewee's families, income or husband-wife relationships. An Indian community is a very close-knit structure where virtually everybody knows everybody else and news travels like fire. If the researcher appeared like a 'peeping tom' prying in the interviewees' private lives, it would have doomed the future interviews. So one has to present oneself as a professional researcher whose interests are strictly academic.

For the first couple of interviews, the researcher tried to appear as a professional researcher. In order to eliminate any fear of gossip about what the interviewees would say, the interviewees were furnished with a signed statement stating that the information provided by them would be used strictly for academic purposes. Giving out these statements was stopped after four or five interviews when it was felt that interviewees had developed enough confidence in the researcher. The interviewer was well aware that she was studying a group which is very close-knit in terms of communication network. The researcher knew that if the interviewees felt that questions were too personal or that the researcher would gossip about their answers, these feelings would be conveyed to other members of the community and the possibility of getting further interviews would be doomed forever. So the researcher was very careful to avoid seemingly "personal" questions and to convey the impression that the answers given would be totally confidential. Besides, the questions were designed to appear to probe the attitudes of the interviewees rather than gather information about their actual behavior in concrete situations.

In order to make the interviewees regard the researcher

DATA COLLECTION

as a confidante, efforts were made to identify with the interviewees' lives and the problems they face in America by telling anecdotes from the researchers' own experiences within the American society. The interviewees were very receptive. They cordially invited the researcher to their house, patiently answered all her questions and then treated the researcher to lunch or tea. The researcher became very close to a few of them who afterwards provided her with further information about the community.

GATHERING DATA

Subjects' definitions of the social situations were discovered through in-depth interviews[1] and to a limited extent by participant observation. The data gathered from participant observation was mainly used to substantiate the information gathered from in-depth interviews. Field notes were taken on the topics of conversations in these gatherings on how the males and the females interacted with each other and among themselves, on the description of the settings and their occupants, on the duration of the gatherings and so on. The data from participant observation were mainly used to describe the interviewees' actual behaviors in concrete situations. For example, the data from participant observation were very useful in illuminating the status competition existing within the Indian community.

The participant observation study of the Indian immigrants involved the researcher becoming a member of the Bengali cultural society and attending social functions such as picnics, cultural festivals and other activities. The researcher also met the subjects informally in social gatherings. In these gatherings, note was taken of what the subjects talked about, who was associated with whom, how the food was served, how the men and the women behaved, how they separated into male and female groups, and what conversations went on within each group.

The data collection also included focused interviews consisting of open-ended questions. Interviewees were usually called over the telephone and an interview was requested. The appointments for interviews were usually given for late mornings, afternoons or early evenings. The interviews were usually conducted at the residence of the interviewees.

SAMPLING

For the purpose of the study, a list of members belonging to a Bengali Cultural association located in a New Jersey area was found. The purpose was to interview twenty-

DATA COLLECTION

five couples. Because of limited financial resources, it
was decided to try to interview all the available couples
with children from the researcher's own area and then go to
the New Jersey area to interview the rest of the twenty-five
couples.

The twenty couples that were interviewed from the New
Jersey area were the first twenty couples who agreed to be
interviewed when approached by telephone. Couples with
children were selected because a considerable portion of the
interview schedule was devoted to the issue of raising
children and the problems faced therein. The method of
sampling used can be termed "snow-ball" sampling since it is
thought to be particularly useful for studying an ethnic
group maintaining some form of formal and informal
communication network. "Snowball" sampling involves
interviewing all the subjects who can be located by ordinary
means such as membership lists of ethnic organizations,
immigration and census records, etc. These subjects would
then be asked for the names of other prospective subjects
with whom they are acquainted, but who may not be known to
the researcher. By repeating this process several times,
most of the prospective subjects hopefully can be identified
and contacted. Since the members of the Indian community
maintain a very close-knit network of communication among
themselves, "snowball" sampling was thought to be highly

appropriate. Thus, the members of the Bengali cultural association were contacted from a list where their names appeared in alphabetical order. These subjects were then asked for the names of other Bengalis with whom they were acquainted.

Snowball sampling method, however, introduces a bias in the study since the cases which cannot be located or interviewed either because they are not listed or because they are not social might bias the study.

Every effort was made, however, to make the sample as varied as possible in terms of age and occupation. The unique character of the Immigration Act of 1965, however, made the sample mostly homogeneous in terms of socio-economic status and educational background. Besides, the structure of the Bengali community somewhat offset the bias introduced by "snowball" sampling. Within the Bengali community, there are smaller cliques consisting of very close friends and sometimes relatives. Efforts were made to contact persons from different cliques and then ask for the names of their friends and relatives. The researcher's long association with the Bengali community helped her to identify different cliques and their insiders.

The complete interview was done in the researcher's native language and the data was taped. The whole interview was then transcribed into English while being translated from the tape.

DATA COLLECTION

PROBLEM OF OVERIDENTIFICATION

A problem of doing research among the members of an ethnic group when the researcher belongs to the same group is the problem of overidentification. The researcher may become emotionally involved not only in his/her study but also with the people she is studying. As Herbert Gans says, this involvement helps her understand the people she is studying and to look at the world through their eyes. At the same time, this involvement can blind her to some of their behavior patterns and thus, distort the study (1962: 343). These problems can be avoided if the researcher is aware of the identification problem. As Dollard says, the rational self of the observer should turn its perceptual engine not only at the outside world, but also at the inside world of unverbalized attitudes which often guide uncritical vision of outside events. The 'self' warned of this possibility may exercise a valuable criticism of its own operations (1957: 31). The other way to avoid the problem of overidentification would be to get away from the interview setting as frequently as possible and look at the data as an outsider. As far as present research is concerned, since the interviews were done mostly on weekends in a location which was within commuting distance and the interviewer commuted back and forth from the interview setting, it was possible to maintain the position of a "detached observer".

However, the problem of overidentification can work both ways. The subjects may overidentify with the researcher in certain aspects and block out information in other areas. In the present case, it was felt that the subject saw the researcher as one of them vis-a-vis American society and really 'opened up' when asked to narrate the bad parts of American society. Had a native-born American asked them the same questions, it is doubtful whether they would have been so eloquent in criticizing the Americans. On the hand, when asked to state the bad parts of the Indian community, they clammed up, presumably for a fear of gossip. It is only when the researcher became friendly with some of the interviewees that they started talking about the jealousies and in-fighting that go on within the community. Since the information was given in great confidence, every effort was made to use that information in such a way as not to divulge the source of information and also to use it whenever it was deemed absolutely necessary in analyzing the data.

DATA COLLECTION

BACKGROUND CHARACTERISTICS

Age and Years of Residence

Effort was made to get a cross-section of people in terms of age. Availability of a cross-section in terms of age was limited by the fact that the people belonging to certain age groups applied for a visa for immigration. Thus, the Indians who applied for visas were for the most part in their mid twenties or early thirties and were yet to be established professionally in India. The age distribution of the immigrants interviewed is given below.

AGE DISTRIBUTION AND YEARS OF RESIDENCE OF THE INTERVIEWEES#

	Males		Females	
Age	N*	Av. Years of stay in the U.S.	N*	Av. Years of stay in the U.S.
20-24	0	0	0	0
25-29	0	0	2	8
30-34	1	7 '74	12	8
35-39	10	9 '72	6	11
40-44	7	7	3	14
45-49	4	14 '64	1	12
50-54	2	17 '67	1	2
55-59	1	2	0	0

*No. of interviewees.
#In the year 1981.

The above figures show that an increasing number of male interviewees belonging to the thirty-five to thirty-nine years age group immigrated during the mid-sixties to early seventies. For the females, the modal age group is thirty to thirty four, which is understandable since in Indian marriages, there is usuaally a gap of five to ten years between the ages of husband and wife. The wives are usually five to ten years younger than their husbands.

Education

The educational level of the interviewees is shown below:

Degree	Males	Females
Ph.D.	6*	1
M.S.	11	12#
B.S. or B.A.	8	8
High School	0	4

*All hold Ph.D.'s in Engineering, with the exception of one who has a Ph.D. in Economics.

#All hold their Master's degrees in the humanities and social sciences except two physicians and one engineer.

DATA COLLECTION   Page 35

   The table shows that the interviewees were fairly well
educated. There were a few high school graduates among the
female interviewees, but none among the male interviewees
since it was impossible, according to the Immigration Act,
for high school graduates to emigrate unless they were
sponsored by thier spouses or blood relatives.[2] Nearly all
the male interviewees received their M.S. from American
Universities. Some completed their M.S. as part-time
students while working fulltime during the day and going to
graduate school in the evening, whereas others were full-
time graduate students on assistantships. Of the twelve
female interviewees, three earned their Master's degrees
from American Universities in social science and one in
engineering. The rest of the female interviewees received
their Master's degrees in India. It is pertinent to note
that since the majority of the male interviewees had their
formal training in the areas of science and technology,
areas in which the demand for manpower is usully high, they
were the ones who were regarded as having 'marketable
skills.' The majority of the female interviewees, even with
their Indian and American graduate degrees, found it hard to
get professional jobs since their training was in humanities
and social sciences. These areas are regarded as highly
competitive in terms of availability of jobs.

The Indian immigrants, who are mostly professionals, were top students in their own country as admission to professional schools like engineering and medicine, for example, is fiercely competitive in India. Some of the male interviewees also came to America as students to pursue higher degrees such as M.S, or Ph.D. and they are extremely bright students in the sense that only the very best could gain admission to American universities for graduate study after applying directly from India.[3]

Occupations

Among the male interviewees, the majority are employed in the engineering field with the exception of two--one is a university professor and the other is employed in purchasing capacity. Two or three of the male interviewees are employed in supervisory capacities and the rest are employed in technical capacities. Among the wives, two are physicians--one was completing her residency and the other was employed in a hospital. One female interviewee was an engineer and another was a college instructor. Two were employed on a part-time basis--one in a store and the other in a library.

DATA COLLECTION

Family Background

The socio-economic status of the family of origin of the male interviewees range from lower-middle class to very high middle-class. The fathers of two of the three interviewees worked as clerks and the rest came from typical middle-class Bengali families in which the father was a professional such as a doctor, engineer, lawyer, government official or a professional in a private firm.

Indian men are generally hypergamous or they tend to marry women from a family occupying a status higher than that of their own family in the society (Ramu, 1977, Ross 1961). Since all of the male interviewees were professional and the majority[4] of them had their marriages arranged for them, their wives come from well-to-do Bengali families. So, the fathers of the female interviewees were engineers, doctors, businessmen, chartered accountants, government officers, a highly placed bank official and a university professor.

Residential Patterns of the Interviewees

The Indian community interviewed does not congregate in one specific locality in that there is not an Indian section of the residential area similar to ethnic enclaves of Italians or Poles. The interviewees were scattered throughout the area in middle-class neighborhoods, residing in houses ranging from $70,000 - 150,000 in prices. The neighborhood is predominantly white with one or two Black or Indian families residing within it. But even in neighborhoods where two or three Indian families were found to be residing, the relationship between the Indian families is very formal. Both the husbands and the wives said that their close friends live in other neighborhoods.

The area in which the interviewees live in New Jersey is a residential suburb of a nearby industrial city. There are a few branch offices in that area of the main industry located in the city. The area is mainly dotted with residential sections, big shopping centers, and a few hospitals. There is also a small community college in the area and the children of the interviewees mostly commute to the city for undergraduate and graduate studies.

The local area of the researcher in which five families were interviewed is also an industrial city. The area is known as the seat of a giant corporation and all of the male interviewees except one are employed in that corporation in various technical and managerial capacities. The area also has a university.

CHAPTER FOUR

BECOMING AN IMMIGRANT

W. I. Thomas, in his discussions on immigrant roles, conjectures that the types of attributes carried over by the immigrants to a new country determine their subsequent behavior. He sees these attributes as determined by the experiences of the immigrants at home, experiences which led them to come to the U.S. in the first place. Once in the U.S. the attributes and subsequent behaviors of the immigrants are the result of the "rational definitions of the situations based on past experiences" (Thomas, 1966: 182). Thus, he distinguished between five immigrant types: the settler, the colonist, the political idealist, the allrightnick and caffone.

According to Thomas, the settlers resolve to break with the past permanently, to seek a home in a new country and to transfer their interests to it. The colonists, according to Thomas, are the ones in whom memories of home are over-determined, who never forget or wish to forget their past, whose allegiances are to their home country and whose superior values are native values. The political idealists, according to Thomas, regard America as merely the instrument of their nationalistic wishes. They are obsessed with the idea of the inferior status of their group at home. Their organizations in a foreign country seek to make that country a recruiting ground for the nationalistic battles in Europe. Consequently, they try first of all to save their members from Americanization.

The term allrightnick, according to Thomas, characterizes the opportunistic types, individuals who realize their ambition of gaining access to some sort of recognition or toleration in the American community by sacrificing the ideals of their own native nationality and family group. This term is usually applied by the Jews of New York city to successful members of their own religion who have found a comfortable niche outside the Jewish community and within the cosmopolitan group of "Americanized" Americans. (1966: 183-188)

The caffones, according to Thomas have the least possible association with any group, ignore their surroundings and accumulate the sum of money they have in mind as rapidly as possible. Caffones are pure opportunists who are unwilling to participate either in the American life or in that of their national group. (1966: 189) The Indian immigrants, as will be illustrated in the following actions, came as colonists. But, in the course of time, they have leaned toward becoming settlers. However, they are ambivalent settlers, settlers who can not totally sever ties with their mother country.

The adjustment of the immigrants to a new country is a 'situated activity' which is conditioned by the types of situations and the trains of experiences encountered by them in the course of their lives in America. The adjustment process is specifically influenced by the factors associated with the immigrants' positions in the class structure. In the case of the Indian immigrants, their economic survival and entry into the middle class lifestyles do not require that they be 'Americanized' first. On the other hand, the life situations of the Indian immigrants make them undertake commitments having long-term significance, commitments which make them virtual 'settlers' in the American society.

This chapter will trace the process of 'becoming an immigrant' for Indian immigrants from their original intentions to their subsequent existence as 'settlers' in the American society. The original intentions of the immigrants to come to the U.S. could be divided into four categories: better economic opportunities, higher professional growth, job problems in India, and to get away from India and see the world.

Economic Opportunities

There was only one male interviewee, who says that he came to the U.S, just to earn money. Money was the main reason behind his immigration to America.

> When I graduated from the engineering college, I worked for five or six years in a small company. Then I started doing business. The business was flourishing. Then I heard from my friends that American consulate was issuing visas. Then I thought, America! I could see the world! I could go there, stay for five years, make Rs. 100,000 and come back. My business was not yet established and I could start it all over again after I came back. I wasn't married at that time. If I had a job at that time, may be I wouldn't have come. I did not have any other purpose in coming except to make money and go back. I do not have any other ambition either, like to become general manager or director....
> (Case No. 13, Male)

Other male interviewees say that they were dissatisfied with the lifestyles they could afford in India, with the money they were earning and eventually decided to apply for emigration to America. Thus one male interviewee says,

> I got a British degree and went back to Calcutta. I used to work in a private company. But the economy started to get worse. I had to live from paycheck to paycheck. At the time of making some extra payments like paying insurance bills or buying clothes for relatives during festivals, you start wondering from where you can get some extra money. I applied to Australia but was rejected. Rumor was that the streets of Canada were paved with gold--you just have to go and pick it up. So I applied for a Canadian visa but did not like Canada. The rule of thumb is that you stay home or you go to a place which is second best in the sense that you would be accepted and you can use your skills.

> I applied for an American visa and came to the U.S. and never regretted it. I knew that I had to work hard, nothing will come easily and establish myself and then expect results. But money craze was not there, never believed that I would be rich overnight... (Case No. 2, Male)

Both the interviewees share the perceptions that America is the land of opportunities and immigration to America would lead to an end to their monetary problems. In fact, the male interviewee in Case No. 2 says that he applied for immigration to America because he heard that the streets of Canada were paved with gold. Other male interviewees also report that they emigrated to the U.S. because they found that living was very hard in India. Some of the male interviewees who say that they came to America with the objective of improving their standard of living are slightly older than the others. These are the people who say that they had a moderately good job in India, at least by the Indian standard, were quite settled and had families when they came to America. These older interviewees say that they knew at the time of their immigration that once they came to America, they would not and could not go back. They say that they had already experienced the problems they had decided to leave behind in India and never thought of confronting them again.

Higher Studeies and Professional Growth

The majority of the immigrants who say that they came to America for higher studies are relatively young. The desire for higher education in America was either combined with the desire to visit the world or was inspired by 'successful people' in India who were already trained in Europe or in America. Thus one male interviewee says,

> All my professors were foreign trained. I conceived of America as a fantasy land. I saw all those people bagging foreign degrees and holding high positions in India. I thought it must be something to go after. I applied to an American university and got a fellowship at _____. At first I thought I couldn't adjust to this society. Thought life was too dynamic. Everyday is different from the other. But after a while I got used to it. Now I don't even notice it anymore. It seems I have become a part of it..... (Case No. 6, Male)

Another male interviewee says, "A lot of my relatives went to foreign countries and came back and were very successfully occupied in India. So I decided to do the same". (Case No. 20) Another male interviewee says, "I wanted to do higher studies here and then go back to India with a very high position."

One recurring theme that runs through these interviews is that all the interviewees who said that they came to America to do higher studies had intentions to go back to India after the completion of their studies. But after the completion of their studies, they took jobs to gain experience. It was the fear of not getting the expected high position in India and also the professional satisfaction they were experiencing from their jobs in the American society that acted as the 'pull' factors which were keeping them in American society. They also say that now they feel that their American training and experience would be redundant in a developing society like India.

To Get Away from India

There is another group of people who came to America because they were bored in India. Thus, one male interviewee says,

> I came because I was bored in India. I did not come for advanced knowledge. When I left the country, I had a good job (was a plant manager). But after working for seven years in the same job I reached a point where I became bored with my job, with my life. I wanted some change and excitement. I got my visa for America but if I had gotten it for Gambacorta, I would have gone there. When I came here, I was prepared to do anything. I knew I had to be flexible. I did not get any engineering job, let alone professional job in the first year. I did odd jobs but never thought of going back.... (Case No. 25, Male)

Another male interviewee says,

> I came to see the world. I did not have any career plans. I did not want to go to college here. I just came to visit the world and then planned to go back. I went back to India but came back because of acute health problems. (Case No. 14, Male)

Another male interviewee says, "I wanted to get away from India and also from my parents for a while."

Thus, these male interviewees left India either because American society seemed very intriguing to them or because Indian society seemed very stifling. The majority of the interviewees belonging to this group were also relatively young when they immigrated to America. They came before they were established in their professional careers.

Job Problems

There is another group of male interviewees who came because they were experiencing job problems in India. Thus, one male interviewee says,

> In 1967 and '68, there was labor trouble. As I was climbing up the occupational ladder, it was becoming more and more difficult to work because of managerial problems. I wasn't getting job satisfaction and the labor trouble was becoming very serious... (Case No. 21, Male)

Another interviewee says,

> When I was working, my company merged with another big company which was pushing its own employees for promotions. I felt I did not have any prospect in that company. At that time American consulate was issuing visas, so I applied. (Case No. 5, Male)

There was another interviewee who initially came to the U.S. to pursue an M.S. and Ph.D. in Engineering, but went back to India twice because he did not get an executive position in America. He also wanted to give his children exposure to

Indian culture. He finally came back to America permanently because he said that the job he was engaged in India was full of tension and pressure. He did not like it and could not take it anymore and decided to return to America.

With regard to the women interviewees, all the interviewees except two who came to America to do higher studies, said that they came because they followed their husbands after marriage. Even the one who came to the U.S. on their own said that they were staying in the U.S. because their husbands are staying here. Out of the twenty-five housewives, five had 'love marriages' or chose their own mates before they were married off by their parents. Even out of these five, only two said they really wanted to come. The other three female interviewees said that they did not have any choice once the decisions were made by their husbands. One female interviewee said that she did not have any role in making the decision but she would go anywhere in the world to accompany her husband. So, the major reason for the female interviewees to migrate to the U.S. can be summarized in a line: "The husband decided to come and I came along." Two of the twenty five female interviewees said that they definitely did not want to come. One says that she did not want to come because she dreaded the separation from her parents. The other says that she did not want to come to America because she hates her life in a foreign country where she has to do all the housework on her own. Her husband held a very high position in India and she could afford all the household help she could get. It is very difficult for her to do all the household chores on her own since she is not used to it.

The majority of the women interviewees, when asked "whether they wanted to come to the U.S. or not", replied that once they were married to a guy who stays in the U.S.A., the did not have any choice. The majority of them, however, say that at the time of their marriages, they thought they would be visiting the U.S. for a few years and then going back. They never realized at the time of their marriage that they would be staying in the U.S. permanently.

One theme which is evident in the interview is that none of the interviewees came because of dire economic necessity. None of the interviewees says that they were unemployed in India at the time they immigrated. The crucial factor responsible for their immigration was that life in India seemed to offer much less than what they expected of it, either in terms of decent standard of living, job satisfaction, professional or intellectual growth, or everyday stimulation. Thus the 'push' factors which motivated the Indian immigrants to leave India stemmed from their dissatisfaction with different aspects of their lives in the Indian society. The 'pull' factors drawing them towards America were their perceptions of the American society as a land of opportunities. These perceptions were consolidated in their minds through movies and magazines and also by people who had been in the U.S. before. These people talked about the affluence of the American society.

In spite of the captivating image of the America held by the interviewees, very few of them thought of making America their permanent home when they immigrated. The majority of the male interviewees report that they wanted to get out of India at least for a while, achieve success, see the world, gain some new experiences, educational or otherwise, and return to India to settle down. So, the composite picture of the immigrants having professional education, at the time of their immigration was a young man or a woman in his or her early twenties, who was just out of college or had worked for a few years in India, to whom life seemed full of potentialities which might not be realized in a closed society like India. Suddenly, there came an opportunity to get out of India and visit America, to which they were exposed through books, magazines and Hollywood movies. Most of the interviewees said that America seemed to them like a dream land or a fantasy land. The immigrants grabbed the opportunity to immigrate to America without much thought about the future. They had a vague notion that they were going to come back to India sometime in the near future. In fact, the parents, friends and immigrants themselves were assured of their return to India once their goals were achieved. They did not have any long term goals nor did they envisage the necessity of having them.

BECOMING A SETTLER

Once they were in America, the immigrants had to work hard to establish themselves. Most of the immigrants who did not come as students had to start out in non-professional jobs. American society was a challenge to them and they worked hard to face up to that challenge and prove to the society, to themselves and also to their folks back home that they could be successful in the American society.[5]

Most of the interviewees who came to America as students were apprehensive about their adjustment in the graduate educational system in America. Others were apprehensive about the difficulties of getting a job. Some were apprehensive about their acceptance by the American society. All these apprehensions were taken as challenges by the interviewees. Most of the interviewees said that they knew they would 'make it' in the American society, but at the same time knew that it would not be an easy trip.

Since most of the interviewees are trained in high-demand fields like medicine and engineering, most of them are quite settled in professional jobs after some initial hardships. Thus, the male interviewees report that they did not have any problem of adjustment. After they got their jobs, things got organized. Professional jobs accorded them all the amenities associated with middle-class lifestyles. Now they can afford a house in a middle-class suburb, can afford cars, other amenities, and visits to India from time to time.

Thus, the Indian immigrants find that they can have access to professional jobs and middle-class life styles in the American society without going through the process of complete acculturation, usually demanded of the immigrants. Therefore, the interviewees report that they find life easier in the American society than what what it would be like in India. They say that they do not feel any pressure to change their distinctive lifestyles and feel that they can live the way they want to. Now, they are so much used to this carefree lifestyle in America that it will be difficult for them to go back and settle in India, although they like to visit India as often as possible and are happy if they can go every year.

In the course of their daily routines, the Indian immigrants start taking on important commitments having long-term significances. The Indian immigrants got married, set up households in America and had children who were to be socialized in the American society.[2] In the meantime, they were securing their own positions in occupations and acquiring skills and training which were suited to jobs in American organizations. They were also building up friendship networks with other members of the Indian community. Thus, they were developing a unique set of ties and commitments in the American society and now are apprehensive about disrupting these ties. Also, as the ties and commitments within the American society were being consolidated, corresponding ties and commitments in the Indian society were weakened.

As the Indian immigrants were learning to handle their lives in the American society, they were also becoming familiar with the "accumulated knowledge of trustworthy recipes" (Shutz,p.321) shared by the native members of American society to interpret and handle the social world around them. As the immigrants became partners in the accumulated knowledge, their participation in the corresponding accumulated knowledge of trustworthy recipes to solve the problems of living in the Indian society weakened. Thus, anticipated problems of day-to-day living in the Indian society now seem gignatic and exaggerated. Consequently, the interviewees are apprehensive about the problems of day-to-day living they feel they might face in the Indian society and feel that they no longer have the ability and the resources to handle those problems. Thus, one male interviewee says that "living in the American society has made us very soft, so much so that we cannot go back and live in India." Another male interviewee says "I like to go back, but I feel that I don't have the guts to go back and face the problems." Thus, India has become a strange place which the immigrants love to visit, if possible every year, but not to go back and settle there. As India becomes unfamiliar and seems incompatible with their current life-styles, Indians, instead of asking themselves 'why stay?', ask themselves 'why go back?'[3] Thus one male interviewee sums up:

> I still have doubts about staying in this country. Feel like going home. But from the practical point of view what I'll do after going to India? It's not that I won't get a job in India. But after ten, twelve years in America, there is a mental change. It would be difficult to adjust, may be within myself. Maybe I'd feel 'why did I come back?' There are many problems of living in India. When I was in India, since I did not see the outside world, that kind of life seemed normal. But that might not seem normal today. I might feel 'I had it, why did I give it up?' It may not be me--may be the family members. When they would not get something, even if they do not complain, I would feel their grievance and that will bother me. (Case No. 11, Male)

AMBIVALENT SETTLER

The Indian immigrants, however, never actually decide to

settle permanently in the American society. In fact, the decision to settle permanently in the American society is continuously deferred to the point where the immigrants do not want to think about it anymore. Very few of the interviewees unequivocally express their desire to stay permanently in the American society. The majority express a faint hope of returning to India in the distant future, "may be someday when our kids are grown up."

The ambivalence about the decision to settle permanently in the American society can be explained if we analyze the following statements:

> As I was born in India, certain things came to me automatically. If I had to know a poet like Dey, I did not have to do much effort. But if I have to know Allen Ginsberg here, I have to make an effort. Then also I wouldn't feel the same. I wasn't born here, I did not go to school with friends who knew Allen Ginsberg. These are the difficult parts of being an immigrant. You cannot be a candidate for election here. I cannot ask for these things from this society being a half generation resident here. (Case No. 7, Male)

The same male interviewee says,

> Very few Americans accept you as their own in the first generation and very few will. We interact with the middle class. But there also, apart fron the professional meetings, there is very little social acceptance in the first generation. Some time, some families might accept you, but there is some barrier somewhere. You are different--you are not born in this town. You don't know what Charlie Chaplin or whoever did here. You can feel this barrier. There are some basic differences--you cannot deny it--it is very much there. (Case No. 7, Male)

Thus, the Indian immigrants, even when they become settlers, feel and see themselves as outsiders in the American society. Lack of structural assimilation facilitating entry into the clubs and cliques of the American society still make them feel isolated. Also, the Indian immigrants are not sure that entry in to the clubs and the cliques of the American society will be very comfortable. Thus, one male interviewee says:

> I don't go to restaurants and movies here, because I don't like the movies here, nor do I enjoy American food. I enjoy going to movies and restaurants when I visit India. Here the nature of my boredom is different. In India, when I used to sit on the porch and watch people, I used to feel that though they are not my friends and I don't know them, they are my 'people'. But here when I see people coming and going, I don't feel anything. Like if there is some accident somewhere and somebody gets hurt, I would go and help and then forget about him. But in India, I would feel curious as to who he is. Where does he live? What happened to him afterwards? But here I feel completely blank. (Case No. 13, Male)

This feeling of being left out or not belonging to the crowd is also associated with a sense of loneliness and boredom. Thus, one male interviewee says:

> From Monday to Friday, I don't feel bored because I am very busy. But on weekends, I feel that life is very monotonous--no variation. The only advantage of living in this country is economic freedom. Apart from that, I don't see any other advantage. I feel I can buy anything but I cannot buy happiness. I have job satisfaction here, but if I could do the same job in my own country environment, I would have felt much better because I would have felt that I am working among my own people with whom I can

do heart-to heart talk whenever I want to.
(Case No. 9, Male)

It is worth mentioning , however, that not all male interviewees report the same boredom. Male and female interviewees who report participation in some organizational activities such as church-related activities or activities related to Indian cultural associations, do not report this sense of boredom. Even the interviewees who are interested in sports or other hobbies do not report experiencing any sense of boredom, although the majority report experiencing a sense of social isolation and a sense of lack of total acceptance. The feeling can be summed up by the following statement made by a male interviewee:

> I don't think that I am a part of this society. Anybody from a European country can come here and blend. But Japanese are Japanese even after third generations. It is not because of society's attitudes but because of us. Blacks are Blacks because of their skin color and also because of their culture. Indian culture is very old. I don't know whether I can get out of this culture and mix with them. I don't even know whether it is possible or needed. Some of the Indians living on the West coast, even after two or three generations, have kept to themselves--lived within their families. There wasn't any conflict between them and the Americans (Case No. 12, Male)

The sense of social isolation is reported by the female interviewees as well. In the case of the female interviewees, the sense of social isolation is more intense. Their husbands have contacts with the outside world through their jobs, but the major points of contact of the Indian immigrant women with the outside world are made through her family members, notably children. Thus a few of the female interviewees report that they do volunteer work in their children's schools, in the neighborhood, church, or in girl or boy scouts. The majority of the female interviewees report that they haave a very limited circle to choose their friends from and sometimes have to be friendly with people they do not like. They complain of monotomy, boredom, and loneliness. They also talk about the lack of real friends with whom to talk openly about their problems, about their worries as to what would happen to their children if something happens to them. The majority of them, like the male interviewees, report a sense of social isolation. Thus, one female interviewee says, "There is no feeling of my country while I am living here." Another female interviewee says:

> We stand out. We wear Saris. we look different I experience a sense of 'I don't belong here.' I don't feel involved here. Sometimes I feel homesick. (Case No. 11, Female)

Thus, the feeling of 'not belonging here' is pervasive among the male and female interviewees. The Indian immigrants still do not quite regard America as their 'home'. The majority of them never actively decide to live permanently in the American society, and continually defer the decision to return so that they can think that someday they might decide to go back. In the meantime, they continue to live in the American society and realize that they have already 'stayed' in the American society, at least beyond the period for which they originally thought they would stay, without actually having decided to do so.

THE ISSUE OF IDENTITY

The feelings of social isolation in a society in which the interviewees continue to stay have also influenced their sense of identity. Thus, one male interviewee says:

> We don't think we have any identity here. We are secluded. This society does not expect anything from us and we don't expect anything from this society. We cannot pick up the values of this society because we cannot get rid of our older values and absorb new values because we were born into our old values. You can have money but you cannot solve this identity crisis because fundamentally it is not your own society. For us it is closed-door society, may not be for our children. (Case No. 7, Male)

The feelings of social isolation and lack of social acceptance experienced by the Indian immigrants are associated with a reaffirmation of their ethnic identity which they feel they can evoke comfortably only within their ethnic enclaves. Thus, one male interviewee says,

> You be as you are. You don't have to follow their culture. What for? We have our own family, our own Indian friends. Eighty percent of my friends are Indians. I am content with what I am. I cannot hide my Indian identity. If Poles or Germans, who are white-skinned, if they want to change their names and identities,

they can get away with it, but not me. (Case
No. 6, Male)

Another female interviewee says,

I feel that I am more respected among the Indian
community, or I feel better among my Indian
friends. Americans see me as Indian. People
who have wider exposures to different cultures
might respect you in spite of your differences,
but people who do not have that exposure
(unfortunately very few Americans do) see you as
an Indian and avoid you. (Case No. 6, Female)

Thus, one male interviewee says,

I'll mix with the Americans keeping my ideas and
culture with me--without changing them, at least
not to the extent which is not acceptable to me
or my family. (Case No. 23, Male)

SUMMARY AND CONCLUSION

The Indian immigrants came to the U.S. to pursue certain objectives they felt to be unattainable in the Indian society. These goals were better economic opportunities, better living conditions, professional growth or a more challenging life. Perceptions of the unattainability of these goals acted as 'push' factors propelling interviewees to try out for immmigration to the U.S.A. The 'pull' factors were the perceptions of the American society as a 'dream land' where these objectives could be fulfilled. Since the interviewees came to America to fulfill certain objectives, they never thought of settling permanently in the American society.

Once in the U.S., the interviewees worked hard to attain the goals that propelled them to come to the U.S. in the first place. The scientific and technological skills they brought with them, their reasonable proficiency in the English language, the opportunity structure, and the manpower needs existing in the American society at that time made it possible for the interviewees to enter the professional job market after some initial hardships. Thus, the Indian immigrants gained access to middle class lifestyles and their entry was not made conditional upon their acculturation. They were not required to be stripped of their identities and cultural values in exchange for that entry. They found their life in the American society very easy and comfortable. They stayed on and started taking on commitments in the American society without really thinking about their long-term significances.

But once they are settled in the American society, the Indian immigrants start to see themselves in the context of the American society. They find out that they cannot blend easily into the American society because of their distinctive physical and cultural characteristics. They find out that they cannot share the lifestyles of the Americans. The Indian immigrants start feeling structurally isolated although they are professionally settled in America.

Thus, this feeling of self-alienation combined with the realization that they can never cast off their Indian physical traits and cultural habits reaffirm their sense of Indian identity. To combat the feeling of self-alienation, the interviewees are drawn toward their ethnic communities where they feel they can experience intense personal feelings and the realization of their Indian identities.

Previous assimilation theories of Park (1921), Eisenstadt (1954) and Stephen Steinberg (1981) assume that economic survival in the American society would solve the problem of Americanization on the part of the immigrants. They assume that assimilation is an inevitable outcome of improved socio-economic status. But economic survival, based on the marketable skills of the immigrants, may also enable them to resist the pressure of Americanization and the accompanying experiences of self-alienation, especially when they come from a cultural mileau which is radically different from the one dominant in the American society.

When the immigrants achieve socio-economic status because of their marketable skills, they can successfully resist the pressure of Americanization usually demanded of immigrants having less marketable skills and being placed in the lower rungs of the social ladder. The latter's entry into the middle or professional classes is dependent on their Americanization. Being placed in the lower class in which they are more susceptible to lower wages and periods of unemployment, they are more exposed to the scrutiny of the formal and social organizations on whose assistance they have to depend from time to time. Improved economic status, on the other hand, makes the immigrants deal with the American society mainly as consumers. They can buy the goods and services needed to maintain their desired lifestyles and insulate their ethnic lifestyles within their homes and communities, away from the scrutiny of the larger society.

The improved economic status of the Indian immigrants also makes the ethnicity of the Indian immigrants a cultural phenomenon. The Indian immigrants are quite satisfied with their economic status within the American society and do not envisage the need for the feasibility of group action to further their economic status within the Anmerican society. Thus, they do not view ethnicity as a means to protect their class status (Steinberg, 1981: 258). The Indian immigrants' ethnicity takes the form of reaffirmation of their cultural identity. They reaffirm their ethnic values, lifestyles and symbols to rebut their sense of exclusion and structural isolation from the American society. Their ethnic values and symbols become a source of pride and group identification and give them the sense of belonging to a group.

Steinberg (1981) concedes that cultural pluralism would appeal to people who are economically well established, but then generalizes that the latter are already assimilated, since groups that have experienced widespread mobility are producing high rates of inter-marriages. This fact is not substantiated by empirical research on economically successful groups.[4] Steinberg's generalizations are based on the assumptions that immigrant groups are usually homogeneous. Thus, his theory, like the previous theories of Gordon (1954), and Glazer and Moynihan (1963) is inadequate because it fails to take into account the diversity of cultural origins of minority groups or diversity of minority goals. For people whose cultural practices are radically different from those of the American society and who cannot easily blend into the American society either because of their physical characteristics or because of their cultural practices, cultural pluralism offers the realization of their group goals or group identities.

Gordon says that cultural pluralism cannot exist without structural pluralism or ethnic subsocieties in which immigrants can practice their distinctive values and customs. (1964) Thus, Jean Martin says that the theory that cultural pluralism is dependent on some kind of structural pluralism which recognizes the ethnic substructures as subsystems of roles and relations through which individuals in our kind of society try to match their inner selves, their identities, with their lifestyles and behaviors. (1981: 152).

Thus, for the Indian immigrants, becoming an immigrant involves becoming a member of an ethnic subsociety where they can realize their inner selves through their lifestyles and behaviors. These experiences are particularly important to the Indian immigrants in a society in which one has to continuously impress and prove to others what one is, a society perceived by them as oblivious to their existence except as workers, and a society whose cultural practices are radically different from their own.

CHAPTER FIVE
CULTURAL SELECTIVITY AS CULTURAL SURVIVAL

Cultural pluralism requires the maintenance of an ethnic sub-society where the ethnic groups can realize their values and identities. Barth states that the cultural features taken into account by the ethnic groups are not the sum total of objective differences, but only those regarded as significant by the actors. Some features are used by the immigrants as emblems of their identities while others are ignored. Barth is thus emphasizing cultural selectivity on the part of the immigrants in order to define their identities.

Kitano, while studying the pattern of Japanese assimilation, noted that cultural pluralism, as far as the Japanese were concerned, involved retaining some elements of their distinctive way of life while discarding others. Thus certain basic value orientations and standards of excellence were retained by the Japanese while others were discarded as unwieldy. In the case of the Indian immigrants it will be shown that certain basic value orientations brought over from the Indian society are retained while others are discarded.

Cultural pluralism, in the case of the Indian immigrants involves selective absorption of both American and Indian values. The selective process, however, should be envisioned against the backdrop of goals of the immigrants. The goals of the Indian immigrants are accomplishment of group cohesiveness within their family and community and occupational success in the American society. The cultural selectivity of the Indian immigrants thus is to be viewed in the right of effort on their part to accomplish their goals.

This chapter will analyze the process of cultural selectivity as cultural survival on the part of the Indian immigrants. It presents a comparative analysis of Indian and American values.

BASIC INDIAN VALUES

Yogendra Singh (1973), a noted Indian sociologist, states from a theoretical point of view, the Indian values of hierarchy, holism and continuity are not consistent with the cultural prerequisites of modernization, westernization. Thus egalitarianism is opposed to hierarchy, atomism is opposed to holism, and progressive evolutionary view is opposed to the Hindu theory of pre-destination. The Hindu view of hierarchy is ingrained into the system of caste and subcaste stratification, as well as in the Hindu concepts of human nature, occupational lifestyles and moral duties.

The Hindu religion book depicts a society divided into four classes: priest, warrior, merchant and servant with the priest (Brahman) having the highest social status. Associated with each caste is a separate distinct set of values and obligations. One's moral duties are the moral obligations of one's own class.

With this, the value of hierarchy serves as the basis of higher status to the elders in the society. Thus age and birth in the specific caste are the factors determining one's status in the traditional Hindu society. The value of hierarchy is closely tied to the value of continuity. This value is manifested through the value of 'karma'. It is believed that social placement of an individual in the present life and its accompanying happenings and sufferings are due to the accumulation of deeds in the previous life.

Holism, another characteristic of Hindu tradition emanates from the principle of hierarchy. According to Singh, holism implies a "relationship between the individual and the group in which the former was encompassed by the latter in respect to duties and rights."(1973: 191) What has precedence here is community and not the individual. This subsuming of the individual by the collectivity has persisted along the line of traditional social structures such as family, village, community, caste, political territory and nation.

The values of continuity, hierarchy and holism are responsible for the development of certain orientations in the Indian psychic. Thus, holism signifies that the individuals subordinate their goals to those of the collectivity. The consideration of growth of the collectivity as a whole should receive priority over that of the individuals. The value of continuity signifies that individuals' positions and their success in the present society are determined by deeds in the past. Thus individuals' failures or successes are attributed to their actions in the past life. The value of continuity gives rise to an attitude of fatalism, whereby it is believed that no matter how one tries, one cannot overcome pre-destination. The notion of hierarchy is the same vein ascribes a status to the individuals on the basics of their birth either in a particular caste or in a particular sequence.

The orientations emanating from the basic Indian values run counter to the basic American value of individualism and a number of other value configurations such as achievement orientations, competition, action orientations and egalitarianism. The value of individualism or self orientation places the individual above the collectivity. Thus, it is believed that individuals, as autonomous units, should pursue their own goals as long as it does not interfere with others' freedom. Hence this leads to the belief that individuals should have unlimited freedom and independence to pursue their goals and should not be hindered by external agents. This is quite different from the value of holism which prescribes that individuals should subordinate their wishes to the welfare of the collectivity. The value of individualism, coupled with the value subscribing competition, signifies that everybody compete against each other for scarce resources such as money, jobs, status and that the best would survive. Thus individual success and failure are attributed to the individual's own capacities and not to one's actions in the past, or to one's destiny. Failure in American society is thus perceived as very self-damaging because of individuals' self definitions as well as outside definitions of themselves as losers. The value of individualism, coupled with the emphasis on competition, leads to achievement orientation. Thus in the American society, one's status in society is achieved rather than ascribed on the basis of age or accidents of birth. Accomplishments and success are measured in terms of money, upward mobility and power and not in terms of how one is fulfilling one's obligations of life, a criterion suggested by the Indian value of hierarchy.

Despite modernization and bureaucratization, empirical studies made by the sociologists like Newell (1955), Lewis (1958), Ishwaran (1966), Vidyarthi (1961) and more recently Ramu (1977), illustrate that the Hindu Great Tradition persists in the rural areas of India. Lloyd Rudolph (1965) says that what has happened in India is a modernity in tradition; where modernity has entered into the Indian character through assimilation and not through the replacement of old traditions. The old values are not completely displaced but there is an accretion and transmutation of forms. Thus, cultural modernization persists along traditional lines.

It is pertinent to note here that the Indian educational system, since it is patterned after the western system, is supposed to be an agent of modernization supporting the western values of individualism, achievement orientation and competition. Singh posits that the educational system of India provides a unique blend of traditional and modern secular values of individualism, liberalism and achievement orientations. Like the persistence of traditional values in the Indian lifestyles in general, the modern educational system in India, instead of supplanting the traditional Hindu values, tends to supplement and reinforce it. The educational system in India tends to reiterate the difference between categorical and instrumental values so that the individuals exposed to modern secular values still cherish faith in the Hindu principles of hierarchy, holism and continuity (1973: 106).

The following section will deal with the responses of the Indian immigrants in the face of the existing differences in value orientations. An analysis of the statements made by the Indian immigrants to differentiate the Indian and the Americans, signifies the cultural features taken into account by the immigrants.

HOW THE AMERICAN SOCIETY OR ITS PEOPLE COMPARE WITH THE INDIAN SOCIETY AND ITS PEOPLE

Americans are seen by the interviewees as extroverted, practical, honest, technologically oriented, very strong and self-confident, self-sufficient, ready to face any situation, hard-working, assertive, lonely and self-centered. Indians, in comparison, are portrayed by the interviewees as introverted, emotional, knowledgeable but not practical, less confident about themselves, lazy and very much oriented toward the family and society. In fact, when asked to differentiate between the Indians and the Americans, most of the interviewees use a definite value judgment to make the differentiation. They criticize the Americans for not having what they consider to be the good parts of the Indians. Thus, while differentiating between the Americans and the Indians, the Americans are criticized for not having family attachments, or not adhering to strict moral codes of behavior, especially in matters concerning sex, and for being self-centered or for being less honest in interpersonal communications.

For example, one interviewee says:

> Indians are much more attached to their families. We visit our relatives to India which is 10,000 miles apart. But Americans wouldn't even travel three hundred miles to visit their parents. We are much more family oriented. They are too individualistic. Community involvement is very low. They care less for others. (Case No. 11, Male)

This lack of attachment is seen between husband and wife as well. Thus another interviewee says:

> The kind of love and respect and affection that we have between husband and wife, I doubt that an American couple will have that. It is somewhat on a commercial level. If you don't say 'Thank you', it means termination of marriage. In that case I don't think, it is much of a marriage relation. In our case, it is more sincere, honest and fundamental. (Case No. 8, Male)

Another interviewee, while comparing the Indians and the Americans starts from the premise that breaking up of a family is bad and then continues that Americans lack a strict moral code of behavior.

> Indian people are happier. The social life and

CULTURAL SELECTIVITY AS CULTURAL SURVIVAL   Page 73

social structure of the Americans are terrible. The family structure, emotional attachment toward each other, moral code of behavior--they lack all these. We are so richer. It is bad because there is no sense in having a family if you cannot keep the family intact. Whatever the Americans do, they break it up. You cannot accept the fact that breaking up a family is good. They are going into marriage, having families, having children and then breaking it up. They cannot make up their minds as to what the hell they want. They have loose morals. Sleeping with a person is not loose morals, but sleeping with anybody is loose morals. They don't have a matter of choice in the sense that "I have these standards in my life" and they have no standards in their lives. If I love a person and sleep with him/her, no problem but these people don't have any qualm about going to bed. That may be an acceptable way in their lives but the problem is it is not. They sit down and talk about it. Oh God, look at this, look at that! If I went there and took my neighbor's wife to bed, my neighbor would be the first guy to come and kill me. But if he would have known and said 'no problem', then I wouldn't mind. The whole thing bothers them as much as it bothers us. But they would still go ahead and do it. (Case No. 25, Male)

Another interviewee portrays the Americans as less honest in their dealings with others:

Our relations with others is sincere and fundamental in nature. When we say 'Thank you' we just don't say it for the sake of saying. We mean it. There is more inner truth in our sayings. Here it is just a formality. (Case No. 8, Male)

An interviewee, on the other hand, sees this vocal expression of appreciation as a good part of American character and worth borrowing:

Although they do too much like saying 'Thank you' too many times or saying 'How are you?' a thousand times, I feel that the Indians could do

> a little bit more and express their appreciation. When I go to India and give good gifts, I feel I would feel better if they express their appreciation. Here also, if you give gifts, most of the Bengalis do not express their appreciation. (Case No. 6, Female)

The differentiation between the Indians and the Americans is done from a value perspective. P.N. Deseu, a noted Indian psychiatrist along with G.P. Coelbo, defines such categorizations as 'blind criticism of the American society'. These criticisms according to the authors take the forms of

> lack of genuine love between adults especially husband-wife, oversimplified explanations of crime, sex, marital problems, mental illness and so forth and stem from a gnawing discomfort with the process of Americanization and the search for a feeling of belonging and an attempt to alleviate attendant anxiety. (Quoted in Saran and Eames, 1980: 370)

From the above statements, it is evident that the Indian immigrants see themselves as more attached to their families than the Americans. In this connection, it is pertinent to discuss the value of family centrism.[1] Family centrism occurs in a situation where the interests and attitudes of the individuals are made subordinate to the perceived best interests of the family. this does not imply that the individuals do not have any concerns for themselves; rather it signifies that the need of the self-growth of the individuals is made subordinate to the interests of the family. Family centrism, on the part of the Indian immigrants, can be explained by expressive, moral and instrumental factors.

When asked to specify the problems of raising a family in the U.S., the majority of the male and female interviewees in the present study feel that without a family one would have a miserable life in the American society. Family, according to the interviewees, represents the only source of emotional security, affectional ties and personal comfort and happiness. Family centrism is also based on moral factors, as far as the interviewees are concerned. The interviewees feel that they have an obligation, responsibility and commitment to the family members. Thus the interviewees feel that they are obligated to look after their spouse's welfare. They feel that it is their duty to bear the educational expenses of their children at least through undergraduate studies, and support them monetarily and emotionally until they are adults. The interviewees feel that they should help and support their children even when the children become adults, although feel that they do not want to be 'emotional crutches' to their children. This sense of obligation is also evident toward the extended family members in India. The interviewees in this study say that they feel they should go to India and visit their parents from time to time. Moreover, some of them state that one of the important reasons for their staying in the

U.S. is that they can earn enough money to help their parents and other family members in India and still maintain their aspired standard of living, something they feel they could not have done in India because of the high cost of living.

One interviewee, when asked to describe the bad parts of the Americans states it is

> crisis in the confidence of their basis relationships, at the basis fabric of their relationships like between husband-wife or between brother and sister. It lacks the intimate touch and confidence. "You have been married for twenty years?" "How could you stay married for twenty years?" If that's the normal reactions then there is no confidence in relationships. You know that you are married to a person for three or four years. If the whole society is based on such fragile relationships, then the society cannot prosper. There is going to have some breakdown somewhere. There is too much greed, too much self-interest and too much self-centeredness. (Case No. 8, Male)

Another interviewee says,

> there is too much freedom and permissiveness and latitude. Parents do not care for the children. They don't set a good example. There is no sacrifice for others and less tolerance for others. Children do whatever they like to do. Parents don't care. Maybe they like families as we do but I don't think that people will hang onto their families at the cost of personal sacrifices. Here someone is 'calling all the shots'. They do whatever they like to do. In our country there is an understanding and personal sacrifice .... Their entire motivation is based on sex. They are intensely ambitious and relatively insensitive. Feeling for others is less. (Case No. 5, Male)

Another interviewee feels that extreme competitiveness

existing in this society is unhealthy.

> These people are always on the run. These people play as hard as they work. Even in their play, there is fierce competitiveness. They are constantly trying to prove and impress others. Whatever they try to do, they do it too much. They don't allow themselves to relax. Even when they are partying, they party to the extreme. They have to drink to the extreme--they have to smoke grass. They have to do it to the extreme. Very few Americans I know of, would just enjoy sitting at home, reading a book or talking to people. (Case No. 24, Female)

Some of the interviewees criticize themselves for becoming too individualistic and self-centered while living in the American society. One interviewee says:

> Here you earn money and then think about how to decorate your house and how to spend it on your wife and kids. In India we are much more attached to others and take part in other peoples' lives. You think about helping others. I don't like the way I live here. (Case No. 11, Male)

In the same vein another female interviewee says "while living here we have become very self-centered. We only think about our husband, kids and ourselves and nobody else". (Case No. 1, Female)

Another female interviewee says:

> When I see myself ten years from now I see myself as becoming more and more self-centered thinking only about my immediate family. I never thought that I would be like this. I don't like myself being like this. I always liked to think about others and their problems. Here when I sleep at night, I think about the cousins and my friends and then think about their problems that I came to learn through their letters. But the next day I become so much wrapped up with the problems of everyday

> life like work and catching up in the household
> work, I forget about all those problems. I feel
> that I cannot go against this current no matter
> how much I try to. I cannot afford to spend my
> time on others no matter how much I try to. I
> feel that this is one of the problems of staying
> in this society. (Case No. 24, Female)

Family centrism, as far as the interviewees are concerned is contrasted with self-centrism or placing one's own interest above that of the family. Self-centrism is seen as too much concern for one's family of procreation without regard for other kin groups.

Cultural pluralism, for the interviewees, involves defining the good parts of the American society which they would like to borrow and incorporating them into their lifestyles. Thus, when asked to define the good parts of the American society, the interviewees mention self-confidence, practical attitudes, sense of responsibility, technological exposure, openmindedness, sincerity, problem-solving attitudes, self-sufficiency, assertiveness, and independence. They also admire the Americans for their resiliency, and fairness in dealing with other people. One interviewee says: "Americans go through a hard life and thus they can survive anywhere." Another female interviewee sees the Americans as very fair in their dealings with others and sees the Indians, in comparison as always inclined to take favor from others. One female interviewee conveys that she had a car-pool with one American and one

CULTURAL SELECTIVITY AS CULTURAL SURVIVAL

Indian lady. She reports that when the Indian lady's turn came for driving, she always called the interviewee and on some pretext such as "car problem", "not feeling well" would ask the interviewee to drive. The interviewee, moreover, reports that the American lady never missed one day and drove continuously for one month since she knew she could not drive the following month as she was expecting a baby. The interviewee concludes "this is American and I like this quality." (Case No. 6, Female)

One male interviewee feels that Indians do not have to follow American culture. Yet he feels that Indians can learn from the Americans their concern for physical well-being. Thus he says:

> You should stay in good shape and be active. Also don't let the past bother you. I have seen in this people that if something bad happens to them, they start all over again from the next day as if nothing has happened. They don't let the past bother them. In our country if two people argue at work, they just don't talk for six months. But here if you have an argument, the next day it becomes o.k. We have to learn to be straightforward, act like a man and not be childish and also to work hard. These people work hard. They know a lot of things apart from education that we don't. They can do a lot of things with their hands like carpentry, drilling. I want my people to learn these things. I don't believe that I have to change my food habit or anything drastically but these are the things that we should learn. (Case No. 5, Male)

Another male interviewee states:

> Americans learn to be independent and learn the facts of life very early. I think we are too

much dependent on our parents--even after we get married and have jobs. If you are independent, you can make a lot of decisions on your own. (Case No. 22, Male)

HOW TO SURVIVE IN THE AMERICAN SOCIETY

The traits that the interviewees think are worth borrowing are the ones they mention as necessary for surviving in the American society. The interviewees say that in order to survive in the American society, one has to be practical, hardworking, sincere, self-confident, assertive, aggressive, independent and economically oriented. These interviewees believe that these traits are demanded by the conditions in which the immigrants live, such as competitive environment, absence of kin and relatives or "your own people" from the society, and the impersonal relations that exist within the society. One interviewee notes this:

> In order to survive in this society, you have to be an emotionally stable individual who can stand isolation, criticism and tremendous frustration. It needs a very strong personality to survive in this society. It is a moving dynamic society where nobody cares for you. You are a forgotten soul tomorrow. (Case No. 6, Male)

Some interviewees say that in order to survive in the American society one must have money. One does not have friends and relatives to help one here and so money is one's best friend.

One interviewee believes that the best way to deal with the problem of isolation is to

> follow an open door policy. We are foreigners here--we are the intruders. We have to be open and accommodative. I think that Indian hospitality can help us a lot along that way. Case No. 8, Male)

The same note is being echoed by another interviewee:

> You have to be flexible and cannot be rigid in your interaction with others. You have to take an upper hand in the interactions in the sense that you take the initiative and approach others. You have to be self-driven. We have a tendency that since we are foreigners, we expect the Americans to come forward and initiate the conversation. If you can overcome that handicap, then seventy percent of the battle is won. (Case No. 15, Male)

The overwhelming consensus among those interviewed is that "you have to be Roman when in Rome." There was also a general agreement as to how you can be 'Roman'. Thus, one can be 'Roman' by mixing with the Americans and by "doing what the Americans do", but not necessarily by "believing in everything they believe in". Thus one interviewee says:

> Basically you have to do what the Americans do. You learn to do what they do, how they do business, how they treat other people and how they behave. You have to mold yourself to this society rather than expect others to mold themselves to your ways. This is the only way you can survive in this society. (Case No. 23, Male)

Another female interviewee says:

> It is not possible that I'd be in America and maintain fully my Indian culture. Now in the house what I'm doing that's nobody's business. But when we are in public we should do what the Americans do. Like we can be more verbal in complimenting others, although the Americans overdo it. Everybody lives here because they find life here more comfortable and they should be more flexible and act like Americans. That doesn't mean that we have to be on dope. American tradition is not taking dope either. We don't have to throw out our culture. We have to know our values and social customs. There are bad things in the society. But there are good things also. You should pick out the good things like learning to become independent, and active and assertive. (Case No. 2, Female)

The Indian immigrants feel that the basic trait they can borrow from the Americans is the value of independence. By independence, the interviewees mean assertiveness, ability to make independent decisions and take responsibility for their own actions. The interviewees' belief in the value of independence is also associated with their belief in individualism. Thus almost all the interviewees say that individuals are responsible for their own success or failure in their lives. This belief is stretched to the point of blaming themselves for their lack of verbal skills in the English language. This lack the interviewees feel, is hindering their occupational growth. The interviewees also believe in competition and achievement orientation. Thus they believe that one has to earn status and prestige in the society; it cannot be ascribed on the basis of caste, age or family background. One male interviewee sees a conflict between the value of independence and family centrism. He states:

> Americans are more dominant in nature. They try to dominate others. More so than the Indians. Indians have stronger family relationships. Here both male and female want to dominate each other which might give rise to problems. We have a tendency to compromise. I think we do more compromising than the Americans. I think it is a good trait, especially in a family relationship. It may not be good in the work environment. In the latter, you have to be dominant. On the other hand, at work it does not do you any good trying to be compromising. So we should learn to be dominant within the work relationship. It is very difficult though. It would be like trying to have a 'split personality'--to be a different person at work and at home. (Case No. 22, Male)

This conflict can be avoided by keeping the home separate from the society. Yet, independence as far as the interviewees are concerned is differentiated from self-centrism when contrasted with family centrism. Self-centrism, which signifies placing individual interest above that of the family is discarded by the interviewees. Thus, the male interviewees report that they have sacrificed chances of promotions, lucrative job offers and salary hikes because they declined transfers, either overseas or to other parts of the country, where their family members did not want to move. One female physician comments that she will give up her profession the moment she feels that it is damaging her family.

The belief in achieved rather than ascribed status and

also the definition of success in terms of money, upward mobility and material possessions have made the Indian immigrants a group of "status seekers" within the Indian community. One's prestige within the community is based on how successful one is in terms of material possession. One male interviewee says:

> In India you could earn less and can lower your standard; nobody will bother or tell you anything. Your lifestyle is flexible. You can adjust your life-style to your income level. But over here there is an established standard of life which you have to maintain. The standard is very rigid and brings in some kind of stress. Nobody has set this standard but everybody in their mind has set it up. Maintaining the standard is very hard for some people. For others it is not. For everybody it is a hardship in the sense that once you reach that standard, the standard goes up. So it is always a hassle. (Case No. 4, Male)

Another female interviewee says that one cannot be friendly with anybody within the Indian community because everybody is fighting for money and status and it breeds jealousy and infighting.

Social status is defined as the ranking of individuals on a prestige hierarchy on the basis of some criteria agreed upon the society or the community. These criteria vary from society to society and from community to community. Thus age, birth in a particular caste, family background are some of the important criteria determining one's social status within the Indian society. These criteria are deemed as irrelevant by the interviewees within American society.

Thus conspicuous consumption, possession of material goods like a big house, expensive cars, maintaining a specific lifestyle have become important criteria in determining one's status within the Indian community. Acceptance of the value, achievement orientation, in a materialistic society has made Indian immigrants measure success in terms of material possession.

This change in the criteria to determine success within the Indian community is associated with changes in other areas of community relationships. The Indian community under study is composed of small companionate circles or small cliques whose members call each other as 'friend'. Yet, the nature of their friendship is quite different from what is defined as "friendship" in India. According to Coelho (1974), in the Indian cultural ethos a friendship is no friendship unless it is intense, deep and enduring.

> Three major values are assumed to exist in the mature Indian friendship. First, friendship represents a close interdependence and interlocking of needs and interests. The question of undue interference in each others' affairs or insensitivity to each other's privacy does not seriously arise. A second basic assumption in the Indian friendship pattern is that there is always time to reciprocate favors and benefits. A third basic assumption is that a friendship cannot, or rather may not be broken. Indian friendship is a life-long commitment. (Quoted in Saran and Eames, 1980: 370)

Desai and Mehta (1979) say Indian friends are able to take up from exactly where they left off, sometimes at an interval of years. Gulf of time or space does not have any inhibiting influence and commitment lives in spite of lack of contact. (Quoted in Saran and Eames, 1980: 370)

In regard to the interviewees, their friendship structure represents the interlocking of needs and interests. Thus, their friendship satisfies their needs for companionship and also involves complimentarity of interests. But the question of undue interference in other's affairs or the question of privacy are very much involved. Thus very rarely would Indian immigrants go to their friend's house uninvited and never without calling beforehand. Moreover, friends are also very particular about not to ask personal questions. Second, asking for favors or benefits is avoided as much as possible. Thus, if any help is needed, the individuals usually spend money and buy the services instead of asking help from their Indian friends. Besides help or favors are usually exchanged instead of just given although in case of an emergency, the community members help each other. The question of returning the favor usually does not arise. In the present study, when the interviewees were asked from whom they will ask for help if they face any problem, the majority of the interviewees answer that they will not go to anybody with their personal problem, but will try to solve it by themselves. Third, these friendships are not seen as life-long commitments. When people move, the intensity of the bonds weaken.

Friends within the Indian community, are not confidants with whom one talks about intimate personal problems. Thus some of the interviewees, mostly females, complain that they cannot discuss their intimate personal problems with anyone except their spouses. The belief in the value of individualism pervading the extra familial interpersonal relationships within the Indian community causes one to regard personal problems as personal failures. The researcher's own experience, while attending a few of the social gatherings gave her the impression that in these gatherings everybody attempts to create the impression as to how happy and successful they are. Thus, it can be concluded that the companionate circles are not the places where the interviewees have their intense personal experiences realized, but participation within these companionate circles gives one the freedom to communicate in one's language, enjoy native food, wear native dress and be a "Bengali".

SUMMARY AND CONCLUSION

Cultural Selectivity, or selecting between the cultural features of both the Indian and the American society is seen as one of the ways of survival in the American society. In a society where individual success has to be achieved and proved, even within one's community, the immigrants must be competitive, achievement oriented and "behave like an American." The families, on the other hand, provide the taken for grantedness in personal relationships and reaffirms their Indian identity. Thus, the interviewees believe in individualism, achievement orientation and competition. The interviewees do not envisage any conflict between their family orientation and individualistic attitudes. Yet in case of conflict, the interviewees subscribe to the wishes of their families and subordinate their achievement orientations to perceived best interests of their families.

The Indian immigrants take into account their family orientations as an emblem of their identities to dichotomize between the Americans and the Indians. In fact they criticize the Americans for their alleged lack of attachment toward their families. Desai and Coelho (1980) view these criticisms as stemming from an uneasy discomfort with the process of Americanization. Ethnicity, thus, is a process of ascription whereby the ethnic groups maintain some distance between themselves and the outsiders. (Barth, 1969)

Commitment to Indian cultural values on the part of the

interviewees remains. Certain values such as, belief in marriage as a life-long alliance, maintenance of the traditional nature of the conjugal relationships, religious affiliation, preservation of native dress, maintenance of the natal language and food habit, practice of physical distance between the sexes are sustained.[2]

Cultural pluralism necessitates some form of structural pluralism. Thus, in this study, the formation of an association named after the specific linguistic community interviewed is noted. The aim of the association is the promotion of cultural values. The Bengali cultural features, given the most graphic expression in the association functions, are the observance of religious festivals, presentation of dance dramas, and musical performances in Bengali language. Cultural features relating to Bengali food, dress, language and styles are also reaffirmed in the association functions. One can witness the practice of sexual segregation in the association functions although strict spatial segregation is not observed and men and women intermittently interact with each other. Yet, both the sexes tend to congregate separately. The association also organizes yearly picnics where the members converse in their native language, eat their native food and dress in their native dress.

The Indian cultural values, for the most part, are

however practiced by the immigrants in their relationships with their family members. Their non-familial interpersonal relationships are influenced by the dominant American values of individualism and competition. Thus, the family appears to be the basic institution which maintains the Indian values of holism and ascriptive orientations. The cultural values which find expressions through the community activities are those which are related to food, dress, performing arts and patterns of sex segregation. Although the Indian immigrants' relations with other community members are influenced by basic American values, the cultural activities at the community level tend to reaffirm their identity as a "Bengali" and reaffirm the cultural feature deemed important by the community members. This serves to draw the boundaries between the insiders and the outsiders.

Thus, the transmission of Indian culture is most effectively carried out within the primary groups such as family, cliques of close friends and voluntary organizations. These institutions strive to reaffirm the regio-linguistic identity of the immigrant ethnics.

The cultural value selected most intensively is that of holism which forms the basis of their family centrist orientation. The goal of achievement orientation on the part of the Indian immigrants makes them accept the values of competition, individualism and egalitarianism. At the cognitive level, the Indian immigrants do not see any conflict between the two sets of value orientations and in case of conflict the ethnic values are somewhat superordinated.

Conflicts are furthermore diluted because the ethnic values of the Indian immigrants are anything but static: The cultural items are adapted and reinterpreted in actual situations depending upon the demands of the circumstances. The following chapters on family and work would delineate the actual situations in which the value orientations of the immigrants have to be translated into practice.

CHAPTER SIX

THE DYNAMICS OF CONJUGAL RELATIONS

The previous chapter noted that most of Indian cultural values are realized within the enclaves of the Indian immigrant families. The Indian immigrant family acts as a carrier of ethnic culture. Experiences of emotional importance take place within the enclaves of the Indian immigrant families. The family, to the Indian immigrants is a place of emotional refuge, a place of intimacy in a world of de-personalized relationships.

Lasch (1977) conjectures that structural isolation of the nuclear family, which enables it to serve as an emotional refuge, also creates unavoidable strains in the form of emotional overload; people expect more satisfaction from the family than it can provide. This emotional overload creates strains in conjugal relationships in an Indian immigrant family because the structure of the Indian immigrant family and the dynamics of interpersonal relationships within the family have undergone changes as a result of immigration. Immigration has brought about

THE DYNAMICS OF CONJUGAL RELATIONS   Page 93

changes in the structural conditions within which the Indian immigrant families have to function.

This chapter deals with the strains of conjugal relationships within an Indian immigrant family and examines how the family members deal with those strains with the help of their 'old world' values. In order to understand the changes undergone by the Indian immigrant families, it is imperative to delineate the nature of conjugal relations as they exist in a typical Indian family.

FAMILY CENTRISM AS A VALUE ORIENTATION

Family centrism refers to the individual's subordination of their self interests to the general interests of the family (Ramu, 1977: 95). Conjugal relations, according to the value of family centrism, would be geared toward the maintenance of the family as a unit rather than toward individual happiness and individual growth. Ramu (1977: 34) says that Indian marriages emphasize the social aspect rather than the individualized aspect of the institution. Indian marriages are thus geared toward recruitment, for the purpose of biological reproduction and also for the maintenance of the family culture. Personal or psycho-sexual gratification is only an element in the general process. The parental role in the choice of partners is one way of ensuring the proper perpetuation of the family culture.

GETTING MARRIED

Most Indian marriages are still arranged by the parents. Thus, Ross says

> In the traditional joint family, parents were morally obliged to find mates for their children and the children to accept their choice. As the marriage was looked on as an agreement between two families rather than between two young people, love was not necessary as a basis for marriage selection nor was courtship a necessary prelude for testing the relationship. The Hindu ideal had no regard for individual taste and in fact rather feared it, as it might upset the adjustment of the bride to her new household. Thus marital choice was subordinate to group end.... Love between husband and wife was the result of marriage in the Hindu view not the prelude to it. (1961: 251)

Ramu more recently notes that his respondents feel that their parents are more knowledgeable and informed concerning matrimonial affairs. But the respondents do have some input in their matrimonial affairs.[1] More and more prospective mates meet each other in an arranged situation, and if they do not like each other, negotiations are brought to a halt. The main purpose of these meetings is to give each a chance to take a 'close look' at each other. In most of the cases, the decision to approve or to disapprove is unilateral, resting more with the boy, although some college educated girls now voice their disapproval of their parents' choice (1977: 39).

Out of the twenty-five couples in the present study, five couples say that they selected their own mates. One couple of the five says that they faced strong objections from their parents to their selection of mates since their mates were from a different caste. The other four couples say that their parents arranged for their marriages although they chose their own mates. The twenty couples whose marriages were totally arranged by their parents, say that the first contact between the two families was made through relatives or through newspaper ads put up either by the wife's or by the husband's family.

SEX SEGREGATION AND CONJUGAL DISTANCE

In the Indian society, the relation between the spouses is the continuation of the established practice of maintaining physical distance between the sexes. The practice is enforced and developed through both formal and informal socialization process. While writing about the Hindu family in India, A. Ross notes that in most parts of India, boys and girls are socialized to separate social life. The physical distance between men and women is maintained by formal means like keeping the boys and girls apart in games and schools. Informal training is accomplished through early indoctrination of the mores of sex role distance. Ross further writes that from an early age, both boys and girls are taught that friendly relations with the opposite sex are immoral. Ross concludes that this training makes it difficult for many young people to change their attitudes and behavior toward the opposite sex even when they grow up. (1961: 240)

This distance between the sexes even after marriage, instead of hurting the structure of the conjugal relationship, helps to strengthen it. Thus, Ross says, "the large joint family supplied the husband and wife with contemporaries in age and sex with whom they could get 'companionship' satisfaction." Furthermore, she maintains that this may have been one reason for their relatively good adjustment for they are not wholly dependent on each other for deep affection or companionship. The wife has her closest emotional ties with her children; the husband with his mother and each has a large group of companions of the same sex in the same household with whom they can share their interests (1961: 155).

Ross concludes that the degree of emotional involvement between the two is low. "A man's relationship with his wife is so natural that he can't describe it. It's a casual relationship with no fuss or emotion about it." (1961:

154) It is a relationship in which affection or love is not necessary for other factors are present which make it durable enough to carry out the function for which it was intended. (1961: 157) Ross's data is being confirmed by Klaus Van Der Veen who says that in an Indian family, though a young wife is emotionally very important to her husband, both of them have to maintain a dignified distance when someone is present, especially in the first two years of marriage. In the presence of others, she is not expected to show any affection for her husband nor does he take notice of her. (1971: 65) Ramu says that

> In the Indian society a husband's conjugal interests in his wife should in no way interfere with his duties to his parents, to his siblings and to other elders of his household. Any display of special interest between the husband and the wife is taken as a sign of a bond that may disrupt the man's filial and fraternal duties and so is highly disfavored. (1977: 75)

Ross's and Ramu's findings about the physical distance between the spouses can be aptly illustrated by the following statement made by a female interviewee in the present study. The situation depicted, however, is an extreme case of physical distance between the spouses, and admittedly is not customary in each and every Indian household, but is nevertheless effective in giving a glimpse of the essence of the conjugal relationship as it exists in a Bengali household.

After my marriage I was living in a joint

family. I had no control over myself not to
speak of my children or husband. My husband had
a very good job but I did not know how much
money he was making. Everything was dictated by
my mother-in-law. I could do things if she gave
me permission. I could not even go to movies
with my husband alone. If we decided to go out,
my husband would first plan to take his sisters
out, then he would take out his mother and then
lastly myself. It might not have happened in
all the families but it happened to me. It
bothered me but I did not think that they were
violating my rights or something--or did not
come to that realization. But it was not very
pleasant. It was impossible to sit with my
husband alone and talk and discuss our own
problems. We were always surrounded by people.
We hardly saw each other alone. (Case No. 5,
Female)

ROLE-SEGREGATION WITHIN THE FAMILY

Parsons (1955) conceptualizes the basic roles in the family as 'instrumental' and 'expressive'. The instrumental role is related to the support and protection of the family and involves leadership. The instrumental leader is the point of contact and articulation between the household and society. The expressive role includes the nurturance of children and the maintenance of the home. The role player manages the emotional harmony among the members of the household. In an Indian household, the instrumental role is played by the senior male. The role set is father-husband. The expressive role is usually played by the senior female, commonly the wife or the household head and the mother of his children. Thus Ross writes that in an Indian household, men are responsible for the financial support and general administration of the family. They supervise the family property. Women are responsible for kitchen work--planning the menu and cooking. Male members are rarely allowed to interfere and are not anxious to do so as household work is considered to be beneath their dignity. It is the mother's responsibility to see that her husband and children are well-fed. Women are responsible for the care and learning of the children. Very few fathers have anything to do with the supervision and training of their children although they seem to take a more active part in their children's studies and education. However, mother is the chief agent through which Hindu children are socialized. The father seems to be too occupied providing the family income to have time for his children. (1961: 249)

Ramu, while corroborating Ross's findings, writes that the roles of father-husband and mother-wife are based on the division of responsibilities relative to age, experience and sex.[2] The father-husband has the major responsibility of protecting, supporting and providing for the welfare of the members of his household. He is expected to direct all his ideas and actions toward this purpose. Ramu, furthermore says that since the role of the father-husband is fundamental to the existence of the domestic group, a certain amount of power and authority is conferred on the actor. The mother-wife is subordinate to the father-husband role. She is expected to play expressive roles within the context of the household. (1977: 84)

FAMILY AND EXTENDED KIN

 The nuclear families in India differ from the structurally isolated nuclear families in the U.S. The term 'family' in India represents a unit larger than the nuclear family in the western countries, especially the U.S. Thus the urban families in India, although mostly nuclear in structure connote "joint family relationships in the thinking, commitments and activities of its members." (Ramu, 1977: 72) Ramu, furthermore, reports that although the rules of residence tend to be neolocal and in the urban areas, kinship ties tend to be based on the respondent's personal preferences, the nuclear family is not isolated. Instead, relations with the members of the "significant kin" are characterized by moral obligations, reciprocal expectations and mutual help. Thus monetary aid to parents and younger siblings is seen as an inescapable moral responsibility. Just as the fathers are morally obliged to assist their sons until they are occupationally settled, so are sons morally obligated to help their parents. Ramu says that such reciprocity is non-contractual and is enforced mainly by social criticism. The help pattern also includes giving of 'soft goods' like care in times of illness, pregnancy and childbirth, consultation in matters related to marriage, and advice in buying and selling property.[3] (Ramu, 1977: 73)

Thus to sum up, the typical Indian family is characterized by physical and emotional distance between the spouses (at least at the initial stages of marriage), division of labor between the marriage partners, marriage defined by the social objective of forming a family and transmutation of family culture rather than by psycho-sexual gratification of individual desires, and relations with extended kin based on mutual aid and reciprocal obligations.

STRAINS IN CONJUGAL RELATIONS IN AN INDIAN IMMIGRANT FAMILY

In an Indian immigrant family, the fact of immigration to a foreign land has caused some changes in the conjugal relations. It has been mentioned before, that in a typical Indian family, conjugal relations are characterized by physical distance between the marriage partners. The husband and wife have their own sets of companions and are not "dependent on each other for deep affections". (Ross: 155) This is possible because of the close ties existing in the Indian society with extended kin. Even when the structure of the family is nuclear, relatives and kin groups fulfill the needs of companionship of both the husband and wife and indirectly regulate the family if it strays away from the accepted code of behavior. This lack of extreme dependence on each other, according to Ross, is the reason for the relatively good adjustment between husband and wife in an Indian family.

The Indian immigrant family members in America lack the network of extended kinship that surrounds them in India. With the exceptions of three families in the sample, all the families state that they do not have any relatives living nearby. Besides, friends which in an Indian society are usually regarded as 'achieved kin' and are labeled as parts of the family and are sometimes more affectionate and helpful to each other than are relatives, are not granted the same status as they are in India. According to Coelho, in the Indian cultural ethos, a friendship is no friendship unless it is intense, deep and enduring. Besides, friendship has to be developed through years of close contact. One's friends are the ones with whom one grows up. (1974) The Indian immigrants in America are for the most part detached from the friends with whom they grew up and are unable to establish close contacts with other members of the Indian community settled in the area.[4] Thus the family members have to depend on each other for sympathetic understanding, recreational companionship and also economic maintenance. This nearly total dependence on each other within the family may cause severe strain on the conjugal relationship and lead to intense conflict. This situation is further heightened in the case of the Indian immigrants because both the males and females were never socialized through cross-sexual friendship and dating. As a result they cannot deal with the opposite sex and resolve possible interpersonal conflicts. The Indian husband and wife, in the majority of the cases, confront each other alone in the American society and make claims on each other, the claims which were taken care of by relatives and close friends in Indian.

Blood has commented that intimacy of contact is one source of family conflict. He says that family members lay all sorts of claims on each other and when conflict occurs within the family, it lacks the restraint imposed by concern for public opinion. (1974: 303) Thus one female interviewee in the present study says that,

> We see too much of each other here because we are alone here. When people are constantly facing each other, they become too casual with each other. This has been happening because we are too much dependent on each other for happiness. (Case No. 20, Female)

Another female interviewee says:

> I know some of my friends have marital problems.

> Here you are too much dependent on each other for happiness and your happiness depends on your spouse's mood. You have no other outlet for your frustrations. If you are in a bad mood, you yell at your husband and that causes frictions. As far as my marriage is concerned, I have been able to retain some amount of newness because I am so busy outside. Where there are no outside interests, marriages may go to the dogs because of sheer boredom. (Case No. 24, Female)

Another male interviewee says:

> My relations with my wife are very close here. But this closeness, this facing each other all the time, it creates problems. When I lose my temper, it becomes fierce. My wife also has no outlet. If she has any grievance against me, she does not get any sympathy from my mother or her mother or her relatives. Here we are closer but our fights are also fiercer. (Case No. 13, Male)

STRESS MANAGEMENT IN AN INDIAN FAMILY

But, in spite of these tensions, very few marriages have broken up. The reasons may be attributed to the built-in stress management mechanisms of the Indian marriages. Ramu (1977: 66) says that Hindu marriages are still looked on as a sacrament, and the marriage partners feel that marriages cannot be dissolved at the mere will of the participants. Divorce is not resorted to as an escape mechanism to deal with the pressures and problems associated with marriage.

In spite of the existence of norms against divorce, most of the Indian immigrants would not have followed those norms

THE DYNAMICS OF CONJUGAL RELATIONS

unless they brought some personal gratification. It is this personal gratification which reinforces the need on the part of the Indian immigrants to adhere closely to values associated with marriage. Thus even when the couples experience a less than ideal conjugal relationship, very few of them feel that their marriage as such has failed.

Both the male and the female interviewees belonging to the present study feel that they have two major roles to play in their families: that of father/mother and that of husband/wife. A considerable number of both the male and female interviewees feel that their roles as husband/wife are inseparable from their roles as father/mother. A good father/mother is also a good husband/wife. Even if the male and the female interviewees feel that their relations with their spouses are not comfortable, they never think of breaking up the family because they have one other important role to play within the family. In fact most of the male and the female interviewees report that although some of the things they do as husband/wife are done as duties, their actions as father/mother are performed spontaneously and playing these roles is very gratifying to them. They enjoy everything they do in relation to their children.

Even if the structural conditions surrounding an immigrant family have changed, the immigrant couples still resort to the 'old-world' norms to guide their conjugal relations. Thus we find that although the conjugal role expectations within an Indian immigrant family have changed, it has not changed to the extent to cause conflict in role expectations. Moreover, in the sphere of division of labor, although the traditional patterns of sex segregation exist, marriages have become more egalitarian with the wives having more to say in the decision-making within the family. There is also a belief that the roles shared by both the husbands and the wives are complementary and the wives' roles are regarded as crucial for the survival of the family by the Indian immigrant husbands.

Conjugal Role Expectations

In order to understand the conjugal role expectations, the interviewees were asked to define "ideal husband" and "ideal wife". The male interviewees defined the ideal husband as the one who is a "friend", a "companion", a "good provider", "open", "loving", "compassionate", one. "who is loving and caring." Some of the male interviewees define the ideal husband as the one "who does not sacrifice the family for professional goals" as one "who keeps peace in the family."

The ideal wife is defined by the male interviewees as the one who is an "ideal mother", "a good homemaker", a "good cook", and "as someone who faces hard times with her husband", who is "supportive", "sharing and caring", "faithful" and "has a pleasing appearance".

The female interviewees describe the ideal husband as one who is friendly, "understanding", "affectionate", "humorous", "smart and educated", "cooperative", "a good companion", "unselfish", "a good provider" and "mild natured". The female interviewees describe the ideal wife as the one who is also a "good mother", "understanding", "supportive", "a good housekeeper", "friendly", and "self sacrificing". She is also the one "who can share her husband's work", "see things from her husband's point of view", who takes care of everybody", and "looks after the well-being of the children".

The wives, however, are expected both by their husbands and by themselves to be "self-sacrificing", "supportive of their husbands", and "good natured". Neither the wives nor the husbands expect the Indian immigrant wives to play companion roles. Thus there is a concurrence between Indian immigrant husband and wife as to the roles both the husbands and the wives 'ought' to play within the family. Thus, the marital frictions within an Indian immigrant family are somewhat diluted because the marital partners share similar ideas about conjugal role expectations. Both partners agree with each other as to the roles each should play within the family.

An analysis of the statements of actual role playing by both the husband and wife would further help to suggest that both the Indian immigrant husband and wife actually play the roles that each 'think' they should play within the family. Thus when asked what they as husbands do which is very important to them, most of the male interviewees say that they try to be friendly and compassionate to their wives. Thus one husband says, "I try to make my wife happy, try to share our ideas, give her little gifts." Another male interviewee says, "I try to be considerate and understanding, support her and shield her from depression." Another male interviewee says, "I try to understand her problems or at least try to see it from her point of view." Another husband says, "I think about my wife--her problems and her desires and try to be a part of her life." Another male interviewee says, "I try to keep relations with my wife alive." Thus there is a major effort on the part of the husbands to establish some sort of support with their wives. They want to establish a relationship of companionship, love and understanding.

As far as the female interviewees are concerned, when asked what they do which is important to them as wives they say, "Apart from earning money, I do everything that needs to be done in order to run a house. My husband just earns money. I do the rest." Another female interviewee says,

> As a wife, I keep the house, cook wholesome meals. When my husband comes home from the office, I try to provide proper food. I also go out with my husband. I try to keep the house clean. (Case No. 6, Female)

Another wife says, "I try to look after his physical well-being. His parents are not here, so it's my duty to look after his physical well-being." Another one says,

> As a wife I stay home and take care of the kids and the house so that he does not have to worry about these things. I took care of my daughter when he went to graduate school. (Case No. 22, Female)

Another female interviewee says, "As a wife, I try to fulfill his needs--biological, physical and emotional. I try to ease his tensions from everyday hassles." Thus the wives mention that their activities as wives were geared toward husband, house and their families.

Thus there is much concurrence between the values and actual behavior of the Indian immigrants with regard to conjugal roles. There is a discrepancy, however, in the roles the marriage partners actually play within the family in relation to each other. Thus the husbands try to play the role of the companion or a friend to their wives; whereas the activities of the wives are geared toward their house and family. This discrepancy, however, does not create any strain in the conjugal relationships since there is general agreement as to the ideas about the roles each should play in relation to the other within the family.

Division of Labor Within the Indian Immigrant Family

According to Parsons (1955), the norms of the division of labor by sex, at least in industrial societies, dictate that the husband is the instrumental role performer and as such is the mediator between the family and the outside world, He concentrates his skills in occupational structures by fulfilling his role as the breadwinner. The wife, on the other hand, specializes in the internal workings of the family and concentrates on keeping the family members satisfied while fulfilling her role as a housewife.

Almost all the male and female interviewees say that they believe in the equal sharing of rights and obligations by both the husband and the wife. At the same time, they say they believe in division of labor. Like one male interviewee says,

> Our relations are based on equality. The internal workings of the house I leave to her. The bigger things, which I don't expect her to do, I do myself. I decide about vacations, buying the house, repair of the house and the car, and I don't expect her to take responsibilities in these matters. (Case No. 4, Male)

Another male interviewee says,

> We are equal to each other. If we want to buy a house, I see about the area, the school district, the church, the shopping center and future saleability of the house. My wife sees where the windows will be, the beauty of the house and so on. When there is a family crisis, we both discuss which way we should go. Like I want to move to the North if I get a better job offer. But my wife doesn't want to move because she hates cold weather. So there is a compromise. In our daily lives, we discuss what has to be done. We are parallel--we are complementary. (Case No. 6, Male)

The male interviewees think that there should be a division of labor based on expertise. There is a general agreement that some household work like cooking, decorating, and socializing children are women's jobs. Whereas vacuuming inside the house, lawn-mowing, taking care of the bills, fixing things around the house are men's jobs. One male interviewee says, "My wife cooks because she is good at it. But jobs which do not require womanly skills like cleaning the dishes or vacuuming--I don't care who does it." (Case No. 25, Male) Another male interviewee says,

> There are certain roles which women have to play like the mother role. Maybe it is because of their physical nature. Father cannot be mother and vice versa. One cannot avoid playing this role at least for the first few years of a child's life. Because of their physical characteristics, women have to be near the baby for nursing etc. (Case No. 22, Male)

Another male interviewee says that mothers should stay home, at least when the children are small, because he does not like "the idea of kids growing up with a sitter. Once the kids are grown up, she can do whatever she likes."

Most of the female interviewees say that they believe in equality of rights but at the same time believe in the division of labor. They say that they have more say in certain spheres of family affairs, and their husbands have more say in others. Almost all the female interviewees say that they have more involvement and responsibilities in the children's affairs, in maintaining the social relations, and in things concerning the internal affairs of the house (like housecleaning and decorating, cooking), whereas their husbands are more involved than they are in the financial matters, in decisions regarding buying the house, buying the car, fixing the house and so on. The reasons given for the husband being more involved in these areas are that,

> Men have more expertise in certain areas and women in others or Mother has to be home at least up to a certain age of the kids, and since they have to stay home, it is only natural that they would be more involved in the household affairs. (Case No. 22, Male)

One female interviewee says, "I am very bad in financial matters, so my husband takes care of that."

Thus in the sphere of division of labor, there in a general assumption shared by both the husband and wife that the roles the husband and the wife play within the Indian immigrant family are complementary to each other and equally important to preserve the family. Both the husband and the wife share a feeling that the males and the females have different areas of expertise, and role playing within the family should be based on such expertise. This feeling of roles being complementary intensifies mutual dependence on each other and strengthens the bond between the marriage partners within the Indian immigrant family.

SUMMARY AND CONCLUSION

Thus we find that the changes in the structural conditions have caused changes in the conjugal relations within the Indian immigrant family. These changes have caused strains in conjugal relations due to the absence of extended kin within an Indian immigrant family. The distance between the marriage partners within an Indian family in India, an outgrowth of the continuation of the distance between the sexes, as it exists in the Indian society, has strengthened Indian marriages, according to some researches. This distance, according to the researchers signifies that marriage partners make fewer claims on each other for recreational companionship, emotional understanding and satisfying the demands of everyday lives. These demands are, however, met by the extended kin and friends in the Indian setting. But immigration to a foreign land, in the absence of kin and close friends, brings the marriage partners for the first time face to face with each other and causes strains in conjugal relations within an Indian immigrant family.

Thus the strains in conjugal relationships within an Indian immigrant family are very endemic to the structural conditions of both Indian and American society. But the marriage partners in the Indian immigrant family resort to 'old medicines' to cure the newly sustained disease. The Indian immigrant couples start out with the assumption that marriage is a sacrament which has to be preserved at any cost. There is a general conviction that a marriage contract cannot be violated according to individual desires. This inclination to preserve the marriage contract is further heightened by the fact that in the absence of 'structural assimilation' on the part of the Indian immigrant, the family unit seems to be extremely gratifying to the Indian immigrants. The Indian immigrants in the American society still lack the access to 'cliques' and clubs or formal or informal associations. Thus family is seen as the only unit which can satisfy their emotional needs and their needs for informal companionship. Thus even if the marriage partners feel that their relationships with their spouses are less than ideal, they have their children to make their familial roles extremely gratifying.

The marital frictions between the immigrant couples are,

furthermore, diluted by the fact that the couples agree as to the roles each should play within the immigrant family. Besides, the division of labor within the Indian immigrant family makes each partner an indispensable part of the marriage and family. Each partner thinks that role segregation along sex lines within the family is virtually role segregation based on expertise, and thus role playing by each partner within the family is practically irreversible and irreplaceable. The male interviewees in the sample, furthermore, think that the mother role is very important for the socialization of the children and thus to keep the family as a unit. Thus, the division of labor within an Indian immigrant family enhances mutual dependence between the marriage partners and helps the family from disintegrating. Thus we find that the family structures of the Indian immigrants are kept together by the common interest and goals developed in working together for family and children, a division of labor based on expertise, and reciprocal relations and mutual understanding between family members. It is to avert the strains in conjugal relationships that the Indian immigrant spouses resort to old world values.

It can be conjectured, however, that division of labor along sex lines has been one of the mechanisms used by the Indian immigrants to keep their families together. The main ingredient that is keeping the Indian families together is their belief that marriage is a life-long commitment and that the breaking up of a marriage is bad for everybody concerned. In cases where the wives are professionally employed, the traditional concept of the division of labor along sex lines is not practiced to the fullest extent. Thus it has been seen that sometimes the fathers are more responsible for child care and carrying on family affairs when the wives have to spend long periods of time in their place of work. Moreover, in these cases, wives are playing more companion roles than 'family oriented' roles. The division of labor along sex lines is more prevalent in families where the wives are fulltime housewives. Thus it can be argued that the division of labor is one of the mechanisms selected by the Indian immigrants to keep their families together. In cases where it is not possible to follow a strict division of labor along sex lines because of wives' employment, it is not followed. The marriage partners in such cases emphasize mutual understanding, friendship, partnership and emotional interdependence to define their conjugal relationships.

The Indian immigrant family, however, is at the same time 'old' and 'new.' It is new because the isolated nature of the Indian immigrant family has changed the dynamics of interpersonal relationships within the family and has put severe strains on the conjugal relationships. Though the survival of the Indian immigrant family is due to its past, the families have changed in order to make room for the ethnic family to thrive in a new surrounding, since too much cultural divergence leads to increased tensions, disorganization, and to ultimate dissolution.[5] The exotic plant of some ethnic institution needs some cross-breeding in order to flourish in a foreign soil. Thus although the division of labor along sex lines exists within the Indian immigrant family, it is based on 'expertise' rather than on age, sex or experience. Furthermore, conjugal relations have become more egalitarian as husbands play more companion roles within the family. The mother-wife shoulders more responsibility and exercises more power and authority within the family.[6] Thus the Indian immigrant family has changed in order to ensure its cultural survival. Cultural selectivity represents cultural survival for the Indian immigrant family.

CHAPTER SEVEN
THE DYNAMICS OF PARENT CHILD RELATIONS

The Indian immigrant family exists as an emotional refuge for its members within American society. It has become a 'haven' of intensive, primary experience in a world of competition and impersonal relationships. In Parson's terms, the family stands as the institution in which relations are determined by 'ascription' rather than by 'achievement.' (Lasch, 1977: 116). But, the Indian immigrant families have another function to perform and that is to socialize their members for a society which is achievement oriented, competitive and characterized by impersonal relationships. The problem confronting the Indian immigrants is how they can combine ascriptive and achievement orientations in the socialization patterns of their children. Both orientations are important to Indian parents as far as their socialization practices are concerned. According to the interviewees, their children have to be achievement oriented in order to be successful in the American society and thus fight the stigma attached to a minority status. The ascriptive values, according to the interviewees, would provide an emotional refuge to the Indian immigrant children from a world of depersonalized relationships and at the same time help maintain their ethnic identities.

Parenting is very challenging to the Indian immigrants because of their ethnicity. Andrew Billingsley feels that race and ethnicity are important variables influencing the socialization of their children. Parents' notions of what is desirable in their children are greatly influenced by their experiences as a Black in a white society. Thus Billingsley writes "socialization is doubly challenging for the Black family for the family must teach its young members not only to be human and American but also to be Black in a white society." (1971: 90) According to the author, it is a constant challenge for the Black parents to teach their children how to be humane and American and Black and proud. They have to teach them to separate being Black and being 'bad' which is the real problem and much harder to separate.

The Indian parents, living within an ethnic subsociety with its own ethnic subculture and occupying a minority status within the American society, experience problems of socialization similar to those experienced by Black middle class parents. Indian parents feel that since they and their children cannot hide their differences like Europeans, it is better to be proud of their differences. Thus they strive to maintain their ethnic identity both for the present and future generations. Therefore, the socialization process is very challenging to Indian immigrant parents. The parents try to teach their children to be American and at the same time to maintain their ethnic values. The Indian parents also teach their children how to deal with the stigma of being a minority in a white society. So following the Black parents, the Indian parents have to teach their children how to be humane and American and Indian and proud. An examination of the parental expectations, child training techniques and parent-child relationships will show how the Indian immigrant parents deal with these dilemmas.

PARENTAL EXPECTATIONS

The male and female interviewees define ideal children as the ones who listen to their parents, are disciplined, well behaved, intelligent, good in studies, independent, obedient, self-sufficient, helpful, courteous, and honest. Thus the parental values display a unique blend of traditional or "working values" and developmental or what Kohn (1963) defines as "middle class values." The Indian parents, on the one hand, want their children to be respectful, obedient and disciplined and, on the other hand, want them to be independent, eager to learn, good in school and oriented to personal growth.

It has to be pointed out, that to the Indian parents the term "independence" has a different connotation from what it means to middle class American parents. (Kohn, 1963) First, the Indian immigrant parents do not want their children to be completely independent of their parents. They say that they do not expect their children to be financially independent when they are in college. In fact, they feel that it is the parents' duty to provide for their children's undergraduate education. However, they feel that their children should work part-time so that "they do not become lazy", "feel the pinch", "understand the value of money", "realize what their parents are doing for them" and so "they develop the sense of dignity of labor". In regard to social and emotional independence, the parents feel that children should be independent in the sense that they do not use their parents as social or emotional crutches. but, simultaneously, they feel that "children should always know that we are there to help them, to listen to them and "children should always know that they can come to us whenever they need any help." By "independence" the parents mean that the children "should be able to make independent decisions," "should feel that they can do whatever they want to do", "should have the ability to fight back" and "be confident in one's self." The parents feel that, although the children should be able to make independent decisions, they as parents should define the broader limits within which the children should exercise their independence. Thus one female interviewee says

> the children can make their own decisions but we have to guide them. We have to define the choices for them. If my daughter wants to be a fashion model, there is no way I'll allow that. (Case No. 4, Female)

Another female interviewee states, "I won't let my children make big mistakes. I wouldn't force independence on them." Another reason why the interviewees feel that they will not condone too much independence on the part of their children can be attributed to their fear of their children becoming too much disassociated from them. One interviewee says, "I want them to make their own decisions but would be happy if they consult us." Another male interviewee says, "I engage my children in decision-making now so that when they grow up they are going to involve us." So the independence, desired by the parents for their children, is seen as an attribute relevant for their children's dealings with the larger society. In their dealings, within the family, the children are expected to be deferent to their parents. Thus, one parent says, "My children should depend on us but should be independent outside." Another female interviewee sums up by saying "I want my children to be independent but not to the extent that we see in Western countries," or "not to the extent that they cut us off completely from their lives."

Thus, the Indian immigrants, while socializing their children, dichotomize between the family and the outside world. They emphasize independence and self-direction when training their children for the outside world and they affirm obedience, discipline and good manners when training their children for their familial roles.

Kohn (1963) says that differences in the parental values are the functions of differences in the conditions of life. Occupational differences are preeminently important in determining the differences in life conditions. He says that middle class white collar professional occupations deal with manipulation of interpersonal relations, ideas and symbols and are subject to self-direction and dependent on one's actions. Kohn (1963) argues that there is a congruence between occupational requirements and parental values of people engaged in different occupations. Thus middle class, white collar professionals expect their children to be self-directed independent, and growth oriented whereas working class parents expect their children to be obedient, disciplined, neat, and clean. Kohn says that this supposition

> does not necessarily assume that parents consciously train their children to meet future occupational requirements, it may simply be that their own occupational experiences have

> significantly affected the parents' conceptions
> of what is desirable behavior on or off the job,
> for adults or for children. (1963: 476)

Since Indian immigrants are mostly white collar professionals, they pay a lot of attention to their children's personal growth, development of their sense of independence, and self-direction.

The Indian parents expect their children to be highly achievement-oriented. Almost all the interviewees said that they expect their children to be high achievers academically. Parental expectation, with regard to children's educational achievement, is also very high in India. But reasons behind these high expectations differ. In India, Children, especially sons, are seen as future economic security. Thus, high academic performance is not intensely expected from the girls. But in the United States, immigrant parents see their children's academic performance as the only tool available by which to fight the stigma attached to the minority status, or, as the only way one can be Indian and be proud at the same time. Thus in the United States, high academic performance is expected from both girls and boys. The immigrants feel that one way to counteract the stigma of being a minority in the American society is to succeed occupationally. The interviewees believe that occupational success makes one's occupational status one's master identity and therefore takes precedence over one's minority status in the larger society.

Since Indian immigrants have succeeded in the American society through academic excellence and, subsequently, through occupational success, they expect the same success from their children through high academic performance. They want their children to be successful in the ways they know they have succeeded such as engineers, doctors or as technical personnel. One male interviewee who is quite well placed occupationally says,

> When we first moved to this neighborhood, we were the only non-white family in this neighborhood. At first people used to ignore us, the kids used to make fun of us. But some people from my company live in this neighborhood and when the people around here came to know of my position in my company, they started associating with us. Then everybody started to mix with us. (Case No. 15, Male)

PARENT-CHILD RELATIONSHIPS

The parents, while establishing relationships with their children, have to be mindful as not to disrupt the delicate balance between independence and obedience in their children's behavior. Thus, in relationships with their children, the parents try to strike a balance between authoritarianism and egalitarianism. Thus, both male and female interviewees state that they want their relations with their children to be friendly, but fear should be present. Like one female interviewee says

> Parents should be treated like parents but the
> relationship should not be such that the
> children cannot open up to us, or in other
> words, Dad is a 'pal' but he is a 'pal' as a
> 'Dad' and not as a 'pal'. (Case No. 12, Female)

The parents say that they try to come down to their children's level and try to understand their problems. They attempt to take an active interest in their children's lives and try to become a part of it. This egalitarianism and closeness on the part of the parents are definite changes in parent-child relationships, from those existing in India. Unlike typical Indian parents, the immigrant parents are not hesitant to express praise and love to their children. These parental role changes, especially the father-role, can be attributed to two factors. First is a belief on the part of interviewees that self-confidence is a very important trait in becoming successful in the American society and too much authoritarianism on the part of the fathers would hinder the development of this trait. Second, the lack of extended kin around the family makes the interviewees realize that they are the only ones to show affection and love to their children. In the Indian setting, although the father is a strict disciplinarian and remote, there are other "father figures" available around the family to be affectionate and lovable. On this point, one male interviewee says:

> Our children are very insecure in this society.
> They have nobody else--no uncle, aunt or

grandparents to turn to. So when we get angry and violent, that scares the hell out of them. (Case No. 20, Male)

Another male interviewee says:

We have to be very careful here about raising our kids. In India you can goof up and still your children come out alright because there are others to make up for your mistakes. But not so here. (Case No. 6, Male)

Thus the immigrant father, unlike a typical Indian father, is more involved in his children's lives and is emotionally and intellectually very close to his children. However, the immigrant mother, like a typical Indian mother, plays the expressive role in relation to her children. But, in America, unlike in Indian society, she is also a disciplinarian. In an Indian immigrant family, both the father and the mother put up a joint front when disciplining their children, although the mothers play a far more important role in the socializations of their children.

CHILD TRAINING

Urie Brofenbrenner has said that working class parents frequently use physical punishment to discipline their children. This is in contrast to middle class which resorts to reasoning, isolation or "love oriented discipline technique." The latter methods rely for their effects on the child's fear of loss of love (1958: 419). As far as the Indian immigrant parents are concerned, they resort to love-oriented discipline more than corporal punishment. One father says,

> I don't spank them right away. I want to understand their problems and try to see why it is a problem, then go for solutions of these problems. I sometimes tell them O.K. kid, if you were in my position, being a father, what would you do?" (Case No. 6, Male)

Another father, however says,

> I try to give love and affection. I care and share. But I feel that bad behavior should be nipped in the bud. If parents are not sometimes hated, they are not good parents. Once they know that parents care, little bit of corporal punishment is good. (Case No. 5, Male)

The interviewees want to raise their kids with 'loving guidance, but they will also lay down firm rules and expect the children to abide them. They like to talk with the kids if discipline problems arise. They are less likely to ridicule or inflict physical punishment because they believe that both of these types of punishment would damage their children's sense of self-worth and self-confidence. These are traits they feel are absolutely necessary for their children to master if they are to succeed in the larger society.

SUMMARY AND CONCLUSION

The above chapter contends that the Indian immigrant

family, in order to make its young members fit for the larger society, has changed its orientations towards its children. Thus in the areas of parent-child relationships, control and restrictive norms have been replaced by discussion and reasoning, emphasizing the values of 'open communication' and egalitarianism. Yet, the Indian immigrant families, especially in the areas of parent-child relationships, are transforming against a cultural backdrop. The immigrant parents do not want their families to be heading toward complete free-wheeling and autonomization so that the families turn out to be critically lacking in social and economic bonds. Therefore, the immigrant parents want to preserve, within their children, a sense of respect toward the parents and elders, loyalty toward immediate kin, interfamilial sociability, and primary relationships structured along kinship lines. Simultaneously, they want their children to be autonomous and powerful in the larger society, overcome the stigma attached to their minority status and be proud of their ethnic identity.

The Indian immigrants, thus, try to combine ascriptive and achievement orientation within their children by differentiating between the family and the outside society. The Indian immigrants want to maintain the separateness of their families because they feel that is the way they can maintain their ethnic identity. In fact, the participation of the Indian families in community activities has been attributed by the interviewees to their desire to reaffirm their ethnic identity to their children. Lastly, the interviewees believe that by maintaining the separateness of the family, they can avoid the disassociation of their children from themselves, especially in their old age. The message conveyed here is that, "You be different from the Americans because we are different to you." Only the future can tell whether they would be successful in realizing their socialization objectives.

CHAPTER EIGHT

THE INDIAN IMMIGRANT WOMEN

The significance of ethnicity, according to Jean Martin (1981: 16), depends upon the interaction between ethnicity and other types of social division such as class and gender. In this chapter, the thrust of the discussion will revolve around the significance of ethnicity as it relates to gender. The chapter specifically deals with the ethnic experiences of the Indian immigrant women.

Previous chapters have emphasized the Indian immigrant family as a secluded refuge from the outside world. Feminist literature (Oakley, 1974, Hartman, 1981, Nona-Glazer, 1976) has emphasized how the seclusion of the family has been associated with a division of labor along sex lines and how confinement of women within the home has resulted in lower status of women in society. In the present chapter, the issues of the family as an emotional refuge and division of labor along sex lines will be examined in the context of the lives and attitudes of the Indian immigrant women. In order to understand the lives and attitudes of the Indian immigrant women in the U.S., it is necessary to delineate some of the background features of the female sample under study.

SOCIAL CLASS AND SOCIALIZATION

The majority of the female interviewees come from upper-middle class families. Most of them are college graduates, although their education was geared toward making them more accomplished and thus, more attractive in the marriage market. Aileen Ross, a noted sociologist, writes, that in spite of the gains in women's status in the Indian society, women in middle class families are still raised with one role in mind, the role of mother and homemaker. Thus, Ross writes "although girls are attending schools and colleges in ever increasing numbers and more young women are taking outside jobs, it is still not a generally accepted idea that middle and upper class women should have careers. The central goal of a girl's life is marriage rather than career (1961: 61). Ross further writes that a number of parents are anxious to have their daughters attend universities. Perhaps one of the main reasons for this new trend is that with the new change from child to adult marriage, the leisure time of girls must now be filled up until they are nineteen or even twenty-five years of age, and college is one way of keeping them busy until marriage. Another reason is the difficulty of finding suitable mates for their daughters. This difficulty might force parents to prolong their education further than they had anticipated (1961). Similarly, Smock says that most women in the South Asian societies choose studies which will enable them to be highly cultivated wives whose advanced degrees will enhance their husbands' social statuses (1971).

The findings of the researchers studying Indian women can be well-supported by the statement made by a female interviewee in the present study:

> It was not my decision to get married. It was my parents' decision. They didn't force me to get married but they arranged it in such a way that I had no choice. They discouraged me from doing anything else. I was sitting at home doing nothing. So I thought that the best thing to do right now is to get married and get it over with. I did partly to please them and partly to get away from them. Because as long as I stayed with them, I wasn't allowed to do anything. After I graduated from college, they didn't want me to get involved in a job or a master's program. So I thought that it is better to get married and get away and then find something worthwhile to do. (Case No. 20, Female)

Another point about the socialization process of the Indian immigrant woman worth noting is the practice of sex segregation. Hannah Papanek (1971), while studying the Pakistani women, observed that "purdah" system is one of the ways in which women's position is defined in a South Asian society. "Purdah" is essentially a Muslim custom of female seclusion. A different version of it exists among the Hindu groups. Papanek says that the "purdah" system can be conceptualized in terms of two different principles: separate worlds and provision of symbolic shelter. Thus, the male and the female worlds are sharply segregated, yet the separation is accompanied by a high degree of mutual dependency between men and women. The concept of symbolic shelter, according to Papanek

> is based on the strongly felt tension between kinship unit and outside world which serves to define home as a clearly demarcated private domain. In a purdah society, women are simultaneously defined as being very important in the family unit, and very vulnerable when they move into the world outside home. (1971: 518)

Purdah provides symbolic shelter for them in the family and also from the strong impulses like sex and aggression.

Papanek writes that sex segregation due to the purdah system has not only created division of labor within the private domains of home "where women work with other women in and around the home at all sorts of tasks", but has also created a division of labor in the public sphere. Thus, another consequence of the "limitation of contact between unrelated men and women implied in the purdah system is the development of a separate female clientele for some services which must be provided by other women (1971: 522).

It is important to note that sex segregation is more an upper-class phenomenon. Improved financial conditions of the family are usually associated with strict compliance with the rules of female seclusion. Lower-class or rural families cannot afford the luxury of keeping their women in seclusion since they have to go out to earn money or work in the fields.

Physical isolation of the women is too traditional a phenomenon for some of the upper-class, modern, highly-educated, urban women in India. The latter fulfill their ambitions in the sex-segregated society by engaging in a profession where the contact with the opposite sex is at a minimum.

Since the majority of the female interviewees in the present study came from upper middle-class, urban families, they were either trained for professional careers or their education was geared toward making them highly accomplished wives whose qualifications would enhance their husband's status. The majority of the female interviewees in the present study say that they came to the U.S. because they were married to a U.S. resident. Only one professional woman came alone to pursue higher studies and then got married to a man residing in the U.S. The majority came to establish a family in the U.S.

LIFE IN THE U.S.

The lives of the Indian immigrant women in the American

society should be seen in the context of the opportunity structures available to the Indian immigrant women and the identity needs of the Indian immigrants which keep the family as an enclave of ethnic values separate from the larger society. The majority of the women in the sample are college graduates. They say that they would like to work outside the home if they can get professional jobs. Some of them did clerical and other non-professional jobs when their husbands were unemployed or going to school, but they are reluctant to do non-professional jobs now just for the sake of earning money, since their husbands are earning enough.

Of the five Indian immigrant women in the sample who work outside the home, two are part-timers in non-professional jobs and three are professionals with degrees in high-demand fields like engineering and medicine. Another female interviewee was going to graduate school and was hoping to find a management level position. Another female interviewee's graduate training was interrupted because of pregnancy and the subsequent presence of a pre-schooler in the household. Thus, only the women who had degrees in high-demand fields like engineering and medicine were professionally employed.

Among the twenty women, who were full-time housewives, three situations can be distinguished. In one situation, five women are staying home because of small children but hope to enter the labor market or do some volunteer work when the children grow up. With the exception of one woman, all the women in this group do not foresee having any professional career. The latter feel that they will have some jobs to "kill" time when their children start schooling.

In another situation, eleven women feel that they are satisfied with their life, feel that they have a good thing going and do not foresee any change in their lives. Some of the women in this group have surrogate careers in the form of volunteer community work. Some women from this group are very active in their own ethnic organizations. They organize religious festivals, cultural shows, India day and so on. Some women from this group say that they never thought of having a career of their own. But a considerable number of women from this group, approximately seven of them, say that if they could find a professional job congruent with their formal education, they would be happy to have a career. But since they know from experience or from watching other Indian immigrant women who have tried for professional jobs that it is next to impossible to get jobs with the Indian graduate degrees in social sciences, they have given up the hope of having a career and are satisfied with what they have. These women, however, are overly defensive about their housewife role. They reiterate that they are not just "housewives" who sit at home and watch soap-operas. Some of them feel that they are doing something valuable by staying home and being good mothers to their children. They feel that their mother/housewife role is as demanding and hard as any professional employee role. There are four women who emphasize that they are very much involved in volunteer activities. They feel that they are rendering their community a valuable service by organizing various cultural expressions such as cultural shows, religious festivals and so on. All the women in this group are very careful to mention their "importance" either as mothers or as volunteer workers.

In another situation, four women went to graduate schools in America. Of these, one woman says that she is not interested in a professional career. But the rest say that they have tried for professional jobs but are unable to land them. These are the women who complain of being the direct victims of racial discrimination. They feel that the reason they are not getting jobs is "nobody wants to hire Indian ladies no matter how educated they are, especially when their training is not in high-demand fields." It is worthwhile to mention that the male Indian immigrants who are professionally employed have also complained of discrimination based on race and national origin. But they say that the discrimination they experience is very subtle and covert. They cannot prove it, although they feel it. The Indian immigrant women with training in low-demand fields view themselves as direct victims of racial discrimination. But these women feel that they cannot fight this discrimination. They feel that going to court is not going to help them, since they cannot prove it. They also feel that they do not have the resources to go to court.

The opportunity structures within which the Indian immigrant women try to locate jobs are very limited, since the majority of the women have academic degrees in low-demand fields. Thus, being prevented from active participation in the professional job market, the lives of the Indian immigrant women center around their families and communities.

The family structures of the Indian immigrants have changed and have become more like the isolated, nuclear family structure prevalent in the American society. The Indian immigrant family is more isolated than its American counterpart since in the majority of the cases, the nearest kin of the Indian immigrants is living ten thousand miles away. The absence of kin has put tremendous pressure on conjugal relations, but the marriages have survived. The changing family structures of the Indian immigrants is also accompanied by several changes in the lives of the Indian immigrant women such as the loss of a female world and improved status of the Indian immigrant women within their families.

Loss of Female World

In India, as has been pointed out before, the husband and the wife live in a sex-segregated world. Both before and after marriage, the Indian women spend most of their time in the company of other women. Before marriage, she goes to single-sex schools or colleges. Even where the colleges are coeducational, the girl students usually interact within an all-female circle of friends. After marriage, the Indian women usually find a set of women their own age at their in-law's place and spend their time with them. Their lives, for the most part, are spent within this female world. The female companions take care of their emotional, recreational and companionship needs.

When the Indian women get married to men residing in America, they leave behind their world of kin and female companions and come to America to set up a family. For the first time in their lives, they face a man, mostly a total stranger, without the support system provided by the other female members of her family. She has to learn to get used to a world which revolves around her husband.

It should be pointed out that the female world is lost

forever to the Indian immigrant women. The Indian immigrant women cannot form a female world composed of other Indian immigrant women in the American society because significant kin are absent from the American society. Second, friendship in the Indian cultural ethos is characterized by long-established, enduring and intense interpersonal relationships. Thus, the close friends with whom the Indian immigrant women grew up, are absent from the American society. Marriage has disrupted their world of interpersonal relationships. Third, the Indian immigrant woman in the American society acts as a member of her family which is engaged in status competition with other Indian families. In the sex-segregated world existing in India, the Indian women interact with other women, mostly her significant kin and close friends, as women in different capacities like mother, wife, worker, professional, kin, friend and so on. Her husband's status does not impinge on her female world in the sense that it does not define her relationships with other females. But in the American society, she acts as a member of her family which acts as a unit. Her world is engulfed within her family in the sense that all her energy, time and identity are engulfed within her family. Since her family is engaged in status competition, her relationships with other female members of the Indian community are mediated by this status competition. Thus, the Indian immigrant women, like their American counterparts, are involved in the effort to "keep up with the Joneses". They lose their female world and with it their separate existences as "women" apart from their families.

Status Improvement

The loss of the female world, however, is compensated by the corresponding gain in the form of improved status within her family. Ramu says that in India, a wife is dependent on her husband for several reasons. First, in terms of age and experience, a husband is quite senior to her. Second, in a household where there are in-laws and kin, the wife's security and confidence are derived from her relations with her husband. Third, a wife's economic dependence on her husband gives her a lower status in the hierarchy of relationships (1977: 89).

In the American setting, the status of an immigrant Indian wife within the family improves because of several reasons. In an immigrant family, although the wife is economically dependent on her husband, the husband is more dependent emotionally, socially and physically on his wife more than if he had stayed in India. The sole responsibility of running the family falls on the shoulders of the Indian immigrant woman, whereas in India, the responsibility is shared with other kin. The Indian immigrant woman's contribution to the family is emotional, social and sometimes monetary. The majority of the Indian immigrant women immigrated to the U.S. when their husbands were either struggling to establish themselves in the initial stages of their careers or were going to graduate school. At that stage, some of the Indian women worked to support the family while others were singlehandedly taking care of their families so that their husbands could spend more time and energy on their jobs. Without the help of extended kin, the husbands have to depend more on their wives for their own physical well-being.

This dependence on the part of the husbands on their wives has made the latter indispensable parts of the families. The realization of their importance within their families coupled with their freedom from the dictates of the elders in the family have raised the women's sense of independence and has changed their relationships with their husbands. Thus, one female interviewee says,

> In the U.S., if I have a problem with what my husband wants or what my husband does, I feel that I have a right to do something about it, whereas, in India, I have to bow down my head and accept what he hands out. If I hadn't come here, I would not have known that I have the right to do something about it. In India, I had no right, no position, I was supposed to have opinions but had to keep it to myself. (Case No. 20, Female)

The same interviewee says:

> When I was newly married, my life revolved around him. But I had to constantly make compromises. At first, it was fun to make those compromises or it did not matter. But after a while, I got tired of making those compromises. At first everything he wanted me to do, I did it anyway, although it wasn't necessarily what I wanted to do. But I did not mind doing it for him. For example, like going to the library with him. I did not mind going along with him while he was studying and I was looking around. But, now, even if I don't have anything to do, I wouldn't go. It would be a big compromise for me. Maybe I was very easy going before--probably because of the way we were brought up. (Case No. 20, Female)

Thus, the Indian immigrant women in the present study demand more independence, a larger share in the decision-making from their husbands, and more respect for and confidence in their decisions. The husbands relent because of their dependence on their wives. Besides, the husbands want to involve their wives in the decision-making because they want to share the 'blame' if the decision does not turn out to be right. Thus, one male interviewee said, "We have to share the blame or the credit for all the decisions we make. We do not have anybody here to discuss things with but our wives."

The wives, therefore, within an Indian immigrant family enjoy more freedom and independence than their counterparts in India. But the independence they enjoy is confined within their families and does not take them to wider horizons. One female interviewee says,

> We can learn a lot of things from them [American women]. We, especially, Indian women, can borrow their courage. In India, the women are not outgoing. They are not supposed to do certain things. They are taught to be shy. You can't do that here. You can't think that since I am a housewife, my job is just cooking and cleaning. Here you have to read and be knowledgeable so that if you go out you could talk and not just sit there. Here if the women lose their husbands, they just don't sit there and expect others to take care of them. They try to go out, get a job and take care of themselves and their families. That's something we should learn from them. It's not up to ten people to come and do things for you--you can do what you want to do. It's something that the Americans learn from the time they are very little. It sticks with them. In India, for very silly little things, people would say that you can't do this, you can't do that. Here, they just do it as long as it doesn't hurt others. (Case No. 4, Female)

The concept of independence has two different connotations to the male and female interviewees. When the male interviewees talk about independence, they mean 'assertiveness' and ability to make independent decisions. By 'independence', the female interviewees mean 'self-supporting' or 'ability to do things without the help of others.' The differences can be attributed to the work experiences of the male and female interviewees. It is very important for the male interviewees working as professionals to be able to make independent decisions. The females, however, are responsible for running the house. So, it is very important for them to be able to do things on their own.

Jessie Bernard says that "how much power a woman might have within her own little bailwick, it has no leverage. It does not add up." (1981: 194) Bernard furthermore says that the status of the non-employed housewife is an example of the disjunction between formal or theoretical social status and actual status. The theoretical status accorded to the homemaker is high, but the social status accorded to the work of the household, including the care of the children, is low. Hence, it is experienced as low by those who do it. An increasing number of these women come to feel denigrated, put down and defensive. Thus, the improved status of the Indian immigrant women within their families has given them theoretical status, but not social status. Their status within their families do not "add up". (1981: 195) The Indian immigrant women are aware of the lower social status accorded to them.

The Indian immigrant women are confined within their own families which exist as ethnic enclaves. But, they are exposed to television and thus, to afternoon soap-operas, evening shows or nightly feature movies. The Indian immigrant women, through the mass media, are exposed to the trend existing in the American society for women to have a right and even an obligation to participate in the labor force. Thus, Alva Myrdal and Viola Klein say that the practice of going out to work, at least part-time, has become so widespread among women in their thirties and forties, irrespective of social class, that those who fail to do so now almost have to give an explanation for staying home. (1962: XI) The Indian immigrant women, despite their confined lives within their ethnic enclaves, are no exceptions. Thus, when asked what kinds of changes in their lives they foresee five to ten years from the time of their interviews, the majority of the non-employed women start defending their housewife role.

One female interviewee says,

> I sacrificed my career for my children. Like some mothers I could have gone to work keeping my babies with the babysitters. I feel that I cannot go to work before my children are going to schools for full days. I don't like that my babies will grow up with the babysitters. Before the children are five years old, some mothers go to work, even some mothers who are professionals. I feel that is not very good. The kind of attention I give to my babies by staying home twenty-four hours, if some working mothers say that they can give the same amount of attention and closeness, I wouldn't believe that. I went to work part-time for one week. I used to come home and get irritated if my children asked me too many questions. I feel that after working eight hours mothers cannot pay enough attention to their kids. (Case No. 6, Female)

Likewise another female interviewee says:

> I feel that I am lucky that I can stay home and be a good mother. It is not possible for everybody. At summertime, when the kids are home, it is a hassle for the mothers. I feel I am lucky that I don't have to deal with those hassles. (Case No. 22, Female)

These female interviewees said that they will have part-time jobs or take some courses when their kids grow up. Thus, one female interviewee says:

> I can have some part-time jobs. I want to have a job where I can do the job and come home in a very short time for my kids. I feel that I cannot go for an elaborate training or education now. That would hurt my kids. (Case No. 6, Female)

Another important point worth noting is that in the American society, the female interviewees have to 'justify' their staying home and not going outside to work, whereas in an Indian setting, the working mothers have to 'justify' their working outside and not staying home, especially if they are working alongside men. The value of sex-segregation is not invoked by the female interviewees in the present study to justify their not working outside their homes. This point is important, considering the absence of sex-segregated jobs in the American society. None of the female interviewees say that they cannot work outside the home because outside jobs would bring them in contact with unrelated men. Their only justifications for staying home are their "families" and "children".

Furthermore the female interviewees' justifications for staying home are accompanied by subtle hostilities to professional working mothers. The latter are defined by the non-employed housewives as "bad mothers", "not too good housewives" and so on. This feeling is understandable considering the fact that accepting them as "successful" would shatter their myth of the value of staying at home for the welfare of their families and children and would threaten their sense of self-esteem[1].

Most of the female interviewees in the present study can be defined as "family oriented" (Lopata, 1971: 64), which blends all roles related to the home, like those of wife, mother, and housewife, into a single "family care package". In the majority of the cases in the present study the full-time housewives say that they cannot distinguish their role as "wife" from their role as "mother."

Besides, the business of keeping the house is seen more in terms of a task-oriented job by the full-time housewives. The performance of the task can be measured by the cleanliness of the house, by the food they serve, and by how well-fed and well-groomed their children are. Thus, the majority of the full-time housewives say that "we work inside just like our husbands work outside. It's the same." The achievement orientation of the majority of the female interviewees who are full-time housewives is very much enmeshed with their roles within their families.

Existing literature on feminist issues sees the division of labor by sex and the isolation of the family as oppressive keeping the women as housewives (Oakley, 1974: 182). But the above data might prove that the division of labor by sex might be upheld by the females themselves to

maintain their status and thus, to protect their own sense
of self-worth in a society which is highly achievement-
oriented.

In a society where the role of housewife is accorded a
very low status, the role players feel denigrated and put
down. Additionally, when the trend of the day makes working
outside the home very respectable, women who stay home feel
very defensive. In the case of the Indian immigrant women,
their lack of skills in high-demand fields in America
prevent their participation in the job market. Lack of
participation in the job market keeps the Indian immigrant
women confined within their ethnic families and communities
and shut off from the larger society.

Confinement of the Indian immigrant women within their
ethnic enclaves has made them very privately oriented
(Turkel, 1977). The isolated nuclear structure of their
families signifies that the Indian immigrant women cannot
share their personal problems with their intimate friends
and kin. Their problems become their personal problems
which they have to solve on their own. The value of family
centrism makes the Indian immigrant women subordinate their
personal needs to the needs of the family. They are
expected to solve their personal problems without
jeopardizing the interests of their families. Since their
involvement outside their families is minimal, they are left

on their own to solve their own problems, a practice which makes them very privately oriented.

Lack of participation in the job market, thus, is seen by these women as their personal problem. They experience a sense of loss of worth as a result of their non-participation. They try to rebut this sense of denigration by defending the value of their housekeeping role and by making housekeeping seem more like a task-oriented job, although they know household work is devoid of any social status. Defending their household role serves a variety of purposes. It protects their sense of self-worth. It also keeps the Indian immigrant women insulated within their ethnic enclave away from the larger society where they are discriminated against because of their ethnic background and are devalued as housewives. Thus, it helps the Indian immigrant women to disassociate themselves from the working women who are mostly American. Circumscription of their lives within their ethnic families makes it easier for them to invoke their ethnic identity and reason that as Indian immigrant women, they are different from the American women, and thus, do not have to follow the recent trend for women to work outside. Thus, the frustration they experience as women by watching the participation of other women in the American society in the labor market is alleviated somewhat by confining themselves within their ethnic families and invoking their ethnic identity. Their ethnic enclaves provide them with ways of protecting their sense of self-worth.

But, their ethnic identity, while protecting their sense of self-worth, does not solve their long-term problems. The more the Indian immigrant women emphasize their household roles and view their household activities in job-oriented terms, the more they are confined with their families. The families as ethnic enclaves further insulate them from the American society and further facilitate their non-participation in the larger society.

Therefore, the Indian immigrant women end up defending the very roles which are the sources of their self-alienation in the first place. Their self-alienation stems from their non-participation in the American society. Their non-participation can be attributed to the limited opportunity structures available to them. But their confinement within their ethnic families further intensifies their non-participation. Their lives remain circumscribed by their families which, existing as ethnic enclaves, are far removed from the mainstream of the American life. Thus, their defense of their familial roles means their defense of the very structures and roles which make them feel defensive and denigrated in the first place.

WOMEN GAINFULLY EMPLOYED OUTSIDE HOME

The experiences of the Indian immigrant women who work outside their homes are somewhat different. Five of the female interviewees in the present sample are employed. Of those, three work part-time as clerical workers or librarian assistants. Three work full-time as physicians or engineers. Female interviewees who work part-time say that they are not very occupationally-oriented and that they will quit their jobs the moment they feel the slightest inconvenience in combining their jobs with their familial roles.

The statements made by the professional working women differ from the part-time workers and also from the full-time housewives (Category II) in important respects. In the area of division of labor, the professional women say that they believe in division of labor along the lines of abilities rather than along 'sex' lines. They say that they do not believe that women have to bear the chief responsibility for family-care and child-care. Besides, they do not believe that women have to stay home because of division of labor.

But, in their day-to-day living, they say that they practice division of labor, although in a modified form, for several reasons. One female interviewee says, "if my husband works at home, there would be tremendous social pressure on me from the community. Another professional woman says, "No matter whether the woman is a professional or not, she has to work in both the places--inside and outside home. We have been raised in such a way that we feel that we should be responsible for housework." Another professional woman says that since she is out in her place of work most of the time, her child is mostly taken care of by the babysitter and by her husband. Her husband is both the father and mother to her child and her child is more attached to her husband. At times she feels guilty that her child is not attached to her. All these women complain that they have to work 'double shift' combining home and job and are very tired most of the time.

Thus, unlike the full-time housewives, the professional Indian immigrant women do not believe that women are meant for familial roles. There is also a recognition that the belief in such sex-segregated division of labor is based on one's socialization and is not a natural phenomenon. Third, they also downplay the importance of mother in child-care roles and believe that a father or a child-carer can safely play that role.

The professional women also differ from the full-time mothers in their definition of their roles as wives. Thus, when they are asked "what do you do as wives," the answers given by the majority of the housewives show that as wives their activities are directed to their family and home. The professional women's statements show that their activities as wives are directed toward their husbands, such as being a "good companion" or "going places with my husband" or "spending time with my husband." In fact, one of them says that "where there is no outside interest on the part of the wife, those marriages must be going to the dogs because of boredom." (Case No. 25, Female) The professional Indian immigrant women believe that a woman's total dependence on her husband can become a bore and thus, a burden to the conjugal relationship. The professional Indian women feel that their professional lives have made them more interesting companions and have perked up their marriages. Thus, the professional Indian immigrant women do not believe that division of labor along sex lines and the consequent restriction of women to the family and home is necessary to keep the marriages together. In fact, confinement of women to the home is seen by the professionally-employed, Indian immigrant women as weakening the marriage bond. But, they are not hostile to the non-employed women and do not denigrate them in any way.

The professional women's relations with the Indian community, especially its female members, is very ambivalent. They are friendly with other female members of the community, but have to interact as "housewives" and downplay their professional lives while interacting with the full-time housewives. Thus, one female interviewee says,

> I cannot share my professional life with other Indian ladies. As far as my profession is concerned, I have to talk with men. But it might create problems. The ladies might think that I am showing off. So I don't talk with the men. I talk with my husband and also with my colleagues about my professional life. With other Indian ladies, I interact as a housewife. It doesn't bother me.

Another female interviewee says,

> There is no support system in my community for my professional problems. The indian community shows very impersonal attitudes. They just ignore the fact that I have a profession. You are respected in this community if you are an excellent cook, keep your house spic-and-span and well decorated and buy expensive furniture and dresses. I feel very left out among the ladies because I am not a very good housewife. (Case No. 8, Female)

Although the full-time housewives within the community define the professional mothers as 'unsuccessful mothers', they deal with them differently in face-to-face interactions. They just de-emphasize their professional identities and emphasize their roles as mothers.[2] The professional women go along with those definitions since they do not want to alienate themselves from the Indian community. In fact, the professional women show difference to the full-time housewives by asking for their advice on family and children's problems. She invokes her professional identity among her professional friends. But, the fact that the professional immigrant women are not given any credit for their achievements in the American society and that their professional lives are ignored by non-employed immigrant women supports the theory that their achievement is very threatening to the sense of self-worth of the non-employed women. The latter deal with that threat by ignoring the professional lives of the professional women and by defending their own familial roles.

SUMMARY AND CONCLUSION

Immigration has brought tremendous changes to the lives of the Indian immigrant women. The Indian women in India are raised to play the roles of mother and wife in a sex segregated world. In this world, the Indian women live within a "female world" within which their emotional, recreational and practical day-to-day needs are satisfied by other female members.

Immigration to America has brought the Indian immigrant woman out of her female world. She loses the world which could satisfy her emotional, social and personal needs. She comes to the American society as somebody's wife and exists as such. Her position is defined by her husband's status. The status competition existing within the Indian immigrant community makes it impossible for her to develop a female world of her own. Thus, in America, the Indian immigrant women experience marital stress as the marriage partners make claims on each other without the support system usually available to them in the Indian society. The lack of the support system, however, increases the dependence of the Indian immigrant husbands on their wives. Thus, the status of the Indian immigrant women within their families improves tremendously.

The improved status of the Indian immigrant women within their families, however, does not give them any leverage beyond their families. It does not add up. Their lives remain circumscribed within their families. But, their confinement within their families does not prevent their exposure to outside information and, consequently, to the trend in the American society whereby the majority of people are engaged in the labor force. The Indian immigrant women are exposed to the fact that in the present society, the achieving women are the "role models". The Indian immigrant women, thus, after gaining an improved status within their families and the position for which they have been socialized since their childhood, feel that this status does not add up. They feel that they have to defend their non-participation in the larger society. Thus, they experience an identity crisis.

Non-participation in the American society on the part of

the Indian immigrant women should be seen in the light of the opportunity structure open to the Indian immigrant women. Unlike their husbands, the Indian immigrant women do not possess skills in high-demand fields. Thus, their non-participation in the labor market is related to the socio-economic forces operating in the American society. But, these women are very private oriented. Their confinement within their families prevents them from viewing their problems in the broader context of the American society. Their orientation to the value of family centrism has made them consider their problems to be insignificant and subordinate these to the larger interests of the family. The dissolution of the female world, furthermore, has made it impossible for the Indian immigrant women to take their problems beyond the confines of their families.

The ethnicity of the Indian immigrants is associated with the seclusion of the Indian immigrant families from the American society and with the Indian immigrant families becoming ethnic enclaves for their members. The Indian immigrant family acts as an emotional refuge to its members. It is also the main conservator of ethnic values. The Indian immigrant women are aware that their roles within their families are not accorded any social status. But, in order to protect their sense of self-worth, they reinforce their familial roles, the very roles which are the sources of their self-alienation. Thus, the Indian immigrant family is an emotional refuge to its members. But, to its female members, it is also the source of their self-alienation.

Ethnicity to the Indian immigrants has meant redefining their cultures in the context of the American society. However, if this redefinition has led to the maintenance of the Indian immigrant family as an ethnic enclave, it has been achieved at the expense of the Indian immigrant woman. The Indian immigrant women lost their world when they immigrated to America, and their gains in American society are minuscule compared to their losses.

CHAPTER NINE

THE WORLD OF OCCUPATION

Work is intrinsically important to the Indian immigrants. In fact, almost all the interviewees say that their job or their professions can be seen as one of the major reasons behind their decisions to settle in the U.S. The interviewees state that their professional satisfaction is one of the major factors hindering them from making the move toward returning back to India.

Sociologists have been prone to make the distinction between the world of work and the world of family. The world of work is seen as a public arena as distinct from the private domains of the family and community. The formal requirements of the world of work are seen at variance with those of the family. The former is viewed as being dominated by universalistic rules of merit, impersonal and formal interpersonal relations and the specialized nature of job performance. The family, on the other hand, is seen as a primary group characterized by affective and personal contact between its members and multifarious role performance of its members. The Indian immigrants, as has

been seen before, view the family as a refuge par excellence
and want to maintain its integrity against the disrupting
influences within the larger society. The values that make
up immigrants' work world in America are seen as detrimental
to the survival of the Indian immigrant family. On the
other hand, their professional life is intrinsically
gratifying to the Indian immigrants. The present chapter
examines the nature of the occupations held by the Indian
immigrants, the importance of the same to them, the
ambitions cherished by the immigrants and obstacles
perceived. The chapter also examines interaction between
work and family life.

NATURE OF OCCUPATIONS AND ITS IMPORTANCE

It has been stated that almost all the male interviewees
are engineers with the exception of one academician and one
sales person. Among the female interviewees two are
physicians, one is an engineer, two are part-time clerical
workers and one a part-time library assistant.

Among the male engineers, three or four say that they do
managerial kind of work. The rest report that they are
engaged in the engineering field, and say that their work is
primarily technical in nature. Two male interviewees say
that they have their own consulting firm.

THE WORLD OF OCCUPATION

The male and the female interviewees engaged in the professional-technical field say that they enjoy the technical nature of their job since it is relatively tension free but challenging. They do not like public relations jobs and feel that their families would suffer if they were engaged in managerial work. They believe a managerial position would demand too much time and effort on their part. The female physicians say that they like their job because it is challenging, involves technical knowledge, and because they love client contacts.

Almost all the interviewees engaged in professional careers feel that they have tremendous job satisfaction. Two male interviewees say their jobs are quite monotonous and they feel that they cannot utilize their full potential in their jobs. Almost all the interviewees with professional careers say that they find their jobs challenging, interesting and conducive to personal growth. This finding corroborates with that of Becker and Cooper who report that:

> Engineers take great pride in their own occupational title, they find the field desirable because of the remarkable skills and abilities engineering training is supposed to provide in them, abilities implied in the occupation's name. (1956: 343)

The Indian immigrants, furthermore, display an orientation which can be called 'cosmopolitan' as against 'local' (Gouldner: 1957). According to Gouldner, cosmopolitans are the ones who have relatively low loyalty to the organization in which they work, a high commitment to their role skills and an outgroup reference. Bureaucrats or locals, on the other hand, show high loyalty to their employing organizations and low commitment to role skills and an ingroup reference. This cosmopolitan orientation on the part of the immigrants is very natural in the sense that, in the absence of any in group reference or a network of friends highly placed in their occupational fields, the immigrants have to depend solely on their technical skills for occupational mobility. Thus, all the male interviewees and also the female professionals feel that their future is in no way tied to their employing organizations. The majority feel that the only way they can move up is by hard work, by "sticking it out", by "becoming productive" and by "not making mistakes".

An analysis of the job orientation of the Indian immigrants can justify defining them by what McCoby has termed as "craftsmen". According to McCoby a craftsman is a responsible family man, work oriented, self certained, self affirmative, conservative and paternalistic. A craftsman does not idolize his work and government. Although he wants to make money, he is motivated even more by the problem to be solved, the challenge of work itself and his satisfaction in creating something of quality. He does not compete against other people but against nature, materials and also against his own standards of quality. A craftsman's main goal is to be a good provider, a good parent, and to create a secure home as an enclave away from work. He is more concerned with being a good father than a good husband (1976: 52). This job orientation is also shared by the female interviewees in this study although they are not "paternalistic". These females are more concerned with being good mothers than good wives[1].

AMBITION

The majority of the interviewees, when asked how far they want to move up the career ladder, answered 'as far top as possible. One male interviewee says that he wants to become the president of his company, another says vice-president. The other interviewees say that they want to go to top technical positions such as senior technical consultant, project manager, director of R & D and so on. The female physicians say that they want to have their own private practice. Some male interviewees say that they do not want to go to the very top if they have to become too involved in their jobs. Others state that they do not want a position which might become too much to handle. The majority say that they do not want to sacrifice their families for their careers and are ready to make compromises when professional and family interests conflict.

OBSTACLES

A few of the interviewees say that they can reach the top by hard work and luck. They state that "if one is good, nobody can stop him". The majority feel that their ethnic background would be a handicap in obtaining the very top managerial positions. This handicap may take the form of experiencing a lack of verbal skills which are seen as essential for effective interpersonal communications. Thus one male interviewee reports, "No matter, whether you have gone to an English medium school or not, you'd face language difficulty in America since you did not grow up here." (Case No. 22, Male) This denial of management level positions because of the perceived lack of verbal skills is not seen by the immigrants as discrimination. They feel that employers are quite justified in not promoting them. As one male interviewee says:

> High positions require client contacts. My accent and my foreign background are my obstacles. The company is not to be blamed because they look after their own profit. That's why they are doing business. (Case No. 18,, Male)

Other interviewees, however, share the view that they

are subject to discrimination in the American society. Thus
one female professional says:

> We have to do something extraordinary to reach
> the top. If my performance level is the same as
> that of an American, I won't get the job. This
> is because of being an Indian and also because
> of the language barrier. You have to sell
> yourself in this society and you can do that
> best if you have verbal skills. Most of the
> Indians don't have that. Besides Indians are
> also very introverted and not very outspoken.
> This is also a handicap. (Case No. 15, Female)

One thing worth noting is that the female interviewees feel
that they will be discriminated against because of their
ethnic background and not because of their sexual identity.
They do not feel that they are discriminated against because
they are females.[2] A male interviewee feels that, although
overt discrimination does not affect the lives of the Indian
immigrants in the American society, covert discrimination
exists and does affect the lives of the Indian immigrants in
the U.S. He says,

> There is discrimination affecting your
> promotions, your salary, your positions in the
> company, your income and sometimes your jobs.
> You cannot deny it although you cannot prove it
> either. It exists in a very covert form and you
> feel it. To get the same treatment, you have to
> be twice as good as an American. (Case No. 6,
> Male)

One male interviewee, who aspires to be the President of
his company says,

> When you are in a technical kind of job, your
> performance can be measured. But when you are
> in a managerial position, the criteria for
> promotion become somewhat subjective. At this

> point national origin makes the difference.
> Most of the Indians are engaged in technical
> kinds of jobs. There has to be a bigger effort
> on my part to move up at the managerial level
> because of my ethnic background. But what I
> plan to do is to work within the system and try
> to change it. I would try to move in a smaller
> company when I would feel that I am being
> plateaued out. But if nothing works and I have
> to stay where I am now job-wise, I would go back
> to India because I feel that if I have to
> languish, I'd rather languish in India. (Case
> No. 24, Male)

The majority of the Indian immigrants feel that since they are deficient in verbal skills and network liaisons, it is not worth trying for management positions. Others feel that since criteria for management positions are very abstract, the employers can easily eliminate the Indians from getting management level positions. The immigrants imbued with the value of individualism, as it is expressed in the American business creed, feel that denial of management level positions to them does not call for concerted action. The immigrants feel that concerted action is not going to do any good. "Things are not done that way in this society. If it is my problem, I have to fight it out." (Case No. 6, Male)

Thus the immigrants feel that individuals are solely responsible for their successes or failures; therefore inadequacy in verbal skills is seen as a failure on their part. Thus one male interviewee, while criticizing one of his Indian friends for complaining about having been denied a position, says, "he should look within himself for his own deficiency. If he cannot communicate properly in English, there is no way he can get an executive position." (Case No. 2) Even where there is a realization that the employers are practicing covert discrimination, the solution contemplated is very private--going back to India. There is a general distrust of the legal system as expressed in the general opinion held that going to court is not going to help much. Moreover, the Indian immigrants cannot justify going to court. One male interviewee says, "if you feel discriminated against and don't like it, you can always go back to India. Nobody is dying to keep you here." (Case No. 1, Male)

A few of the interviewees, however, say that they do not see any problems in their moving up in their company. One male interviewee who says he wants to be Vice President of his company thinks that there is no problem in his moving up. He states that he has to make the groundwork first and that he has reached a stage where his job performance is not that important. But, he has to spend extra hours in his job and that is affecting his family. Another male interviewee who wants to be Director of Research and Development says "my national origin might have been an obstacle at the initial stage of my career, but not anymore. Once people know you, your background does not matter." (Case No. 15, Male)

INTERACTION BETWEEN FAMILY AND THE WORK WORLD

Rosabeth Moth Kanter has argued that organizations of work and the worker's position within it can have a variety of effects on family life. Kanter (1977) talks about several aspects of the structures and organization of work life as they shape and influence family systems. These aspects are the relative absorptiveness of an occupation, time and timing, reward and resources, world view and emotional or the social and psychological dimension of the work. The term absorptiveness has been defined as

> occupational pursuits that not only demand the maximum commitment of the worker but also implicate other family members and command their direct participation in the work system in its formal or informal aspects. (Kanter, 1977: 24)

Thus, a minimally salient and non-absorptive occupation would be defined as the one which involves little of the person, is performed for the pay involved, does not constitute a central life interest for the workers and implicates none of their off-the-job life.

A majority of the Indian immigrants are engaged in technical work and thus there is minimal contact between the family and work. There is also low visibility of the occupation to the family. Most of the male interviewees say that their occupation has not impinged on their family life. Their wives agree with them. The wives do not express any interest in their husband's job and say that they are quite happy with whatever he is doing. Some even mention that their husband's job is none of their business. However, the academician in the sample mentions there is a close contact between his job and family. Because of flexible working hours, he can spend more time with his children. There is also constant interaction between his family members and his colleagues. An interesting caveat is that technical workers express the desire to maintain the separation between home and work whereas the academician wants to bridge the gap.

On the whole the majority of male interviewees say that their relations with their colleagues are cordial but very professional and they want to keep it that way. They do not want to mix their social lives with their professional lives.[3] They want to keep the two separate.

On the other hand the female interviewees report a very personal relation with their colleagues, especially female ones. Their relations with male colleagues are those of partnership. The female interviewees say that they have a few female friends in their work place who are very friendly and helpful. Apart from having professional relationships, they share a personal relationship with them, and are able to discuss personal problems with them. One of the female interviewees says that she is more friendly with her female American friends in her office than with her female friends in the Indian community. Her American friends are very friendly and very helpful to her. Once, when she had a problem, her American friend came and babysat for her; something she feels she cannot ask her Indian friends to do.

Time and Timing

The amount of time one is required to spend in an occupation, and the work schedule that one is required to keep have considerable influences on the family processes. Work related activities can extend beyond the formal office hours and can intrude upon the time the family can claim as leisure which may affect the family life.

In regard to the male interviewees, some of the wives complain that their husbands' late hours bother them. But the husbands say that in order to get ahead professionally, they have to do it. Besides, their professional success also means added benefits for the family. One male interviewee says,

> I have to keep late hours, put in extra hours. Most of the time I have to work on weekends. My goals are becoming higher and higher. I have neglected my wife and children. But I feel that I don't have any choice. I have to do it in

order to stay in the race. But my professional success is going to help my family--more money, more comfort. You can't have it both ways--you lose some, gain some.[4] (Case No. 25, Male)

Two other male interviewees said that they have to make frequent out-of-town trips and that is causing tension in the family since their wives feel lonely. One male interviewee states, "My wife does not like my going out of town frequently but at the same time she wants me to move ahead." (Case No. 11, Male) The majority of the male interviewees say that when they were starting out in the American society, they had to work extra hard to establish themselves. Moreover, some of them were going to graduate schools or were attending graduate school in the evening as a part-time student. The wife-mother at that stage had to assume the full responsibility of running the family and taking care of the children. It was a tremendous burden for them and has made a lasting impact on their lives.[5]

Working hours and schedules seem to be the major problem experienced by the professional women while combining their family and career. Thus one female interviewee says that the problem of long hours is problematic because of its perceived harmful effect on the children. Their long hours of work mean that they have less time left for their families. This has let their husbands make major decisions regarding household affairs. One female professional says,

I have let my husband make major decisions

> regarding family affairs, like buying the house,
> appliances and other household goods. I go
> along with the decisions as long as it does not
> create a major conflict in my thought process.
> When it does, then I sit down to discuss. I
> would rather spend my time at home with my
> children rather than bother with family matters.
> (Case No. 15, Female)

Thus, timing is seen by the female professionals as a problem because of its perceived effect on the children and not on conjugal relations as such. The female professionals are not concerned that their jobs leave them less time to spend with their husband or on house-care. It shows that they are more concerned with their roles as a mother rather than as wife. This concern may be attributed to the fact that the majority of the female professionals have young children.

Reward and Resources

The rewards and resources generated by the job have important effects on the life styles and family patterns. Kanter says, "income helps to determine life style and consumption level, it also determines very directly the relative resources over which each family member has initial control." (1977: 39).

Scanzoni (1970) argues that economic and psychic income from the job affects the presence or absence of marital tension. Kanter summarizing Scanzoni's thesis says,

> there is an overlap or linkage between the economic and conjugal system mediated by male occupational role. The more a man is integrated into the occupational structure, as measured objectively by his occupational status, education and income, the greater is the cohesiveness of the family and satisfaction with the husband-wife relationships since the husband brings status and income into the family in exchange for services and positive feelings. (1977: 40)

Moreover, the more the husband provides in the ways of prestige and education the more the wives are positively oriented. One criticism leveled against this theory is that it leaves out factors such as cultural traditions, values, love and affection which are not captured by the simple economic exchange framework.

The female interviewees in this sample express their contentment with the lifestyle and consumption level generated by their husband's income. They say that they are proud of their husband's accomplishments. One female interviewee states that when she compares her lifestyle with that of friends in the Indian community, she considers herself lucky that her husband earns so much.

The reward and resources earned by the female professionals have improved the family's economic and social position within the community. Thus their professional careers are encouraged by the husbands. The majority of the husbands say that if their wives have talent, they can do whatever they like. They would encourage them to cultivate their skills. But they would not like their wives to work 'as a clerk in a dime store.'[6]

Maintaining a middle-class standard of living is very important to the Indian immigrants. The Indian immigrants believe that they can avert the stigma attached to a minority status by maintaining a middle class lifestyle and a corresponding consumption level. The pressure to maintain a specific lifestyle has generated tremendous competition within the immigrant community. The lack of social contact with Americans has made other members of the Indian community one's reference group. This group serves as a measuring rod to gauge one's status within the society. The pressure "to keep up with the Joneses" according to some interviewees, has bred jealousy and infighting which has hampered the development of a sense of unity. Thus, one female interviewee says that it is impossible to be friendly with anybody within the community because 'everybody is busy struggling to keep his or her own status'.[7] (Case No. 15, Female)

The control over 'exchangeable' resources not only brings status and prestige to the immigrants, but it also insulates them from the disapprobation of the larger society. The Indian immigrants are well aware that their ethnic lifestyle, dress and language are possible subjects

THE WORLD OF OCCUPATION   Page 177

of derision if these are laid open to the larger society. One female interviewee says, "what we are doing inside our home should be nobody's business." (Case No. 2, Female) The immigrants feel that control over exchangeable resources makes it possible for them to insulate their lifestyles. Because of their white collar professional jobs, which are relatively well-paying and stable, the Indian immigrants do not have to approach any outside agency for assistance and thus subject their ethnic lifestyle to external scrutiny. This issue is very important since the Indian immigrants want to maintain their ethnic lifestyle within their families but are not prepared to be stigmatized on account of it.

OCCUPATION AND WORLD VIEW

Occupation according to Kanter generates a characteristic outlook in the world because of the conditions in which they occur. (1977: 42) Hughes (1958), one of the outstanding scholars in this area, remarks that the individual's work provides a subculture and identity which become part of their personalities. The culture, technique, etiquette and skill of the profession appear as personality traits in the individual. In order to understand the influence of occupations on an individual's world view, we have to first delineate the world view generally maintained by the occupational world in an American society.

Two important values, which the American business creed shares with the broad American heritage, are those of individualism and the importance of work. There is a confidence sustained in the American society that work in an occupation "may itself be a legitimate and rewarding focus of man's best energies and not merely a means to higher things." (Sutton, 1956: 276) This viewpoint provides a natural background for an ideology extolling the importance of work and productivity. The business creed supports active pursuit of material wealth through productivity. This creed emphasizes activity and effort on the part of the individuals geared toward high valuations of rationality and progress.

Individualism has two main aspects, an injunction of responsibility and affirmation of freedom. It involves responsibility in the sense that each individual should be responsible for his own actions and accept the consequence of his actions. Secondly, individualism asserts the desirability of autonomous choice by individuals in their own interests (Sutton et al., 1956: 251).

Gans distinguishes between two classes of individualism: object oriented individualism and person oriented individualism. Object oriented individualism involves striving toward the achievement of an 'object'. This may be a moral object or a principle; an ideological object such as 'understanding', a material object such as level of income, a cultural object such as style of life or a social object such as career or status position. Person oriented individualism, according to Gans is based on the desire to be a person within a group, to be liked and noticed by members of a group whom one likes and notices in turn. Thus, person oriented people, according to Gans

> do not seek status by clearly identified and universally accepted status symbols but want to be able to shine as individuals within the group ... and want to act in a way that earns no opprobrium from the group and that fits group beliefs. (1956: 89-93)

It has been mentioned before that the traits of individualism and egalitarianism are contrary to the Indian values of holism and hierarchy. Therefore, it can be safely assumed that the traits of individualism and egalitarianism, portrayed by Indian immigrants can be attributed to their 'secondary socialization' within American society. Since the interviewees mention that their occupation is their main medium of contact with American society, the development of these traits can be attributed to their occupational experience within the American society. The Indian educational system, patterned after the western system of education, somewhat propounds the values of egalitarianism and individualism. Yet the system also distinguishes between 'categorical values' and 'instrumental values' (Singh, 1973: 106). Indian students, even if they are individualistic, competitive, and egalitarian in their educational and occupational lives, do not display these values in interpersonal relations and in their social lives. The value of hierarchy is ingrained in the Indian lifestyle, and influences interpersonal relations in all aspects of Indian social life. The traits on the basis of which deference is paid to superiors, differ from situation to situation, depending on the relevance of the trait to the situation.[8] As for example, in an occupational situation deference is paid on the basis of occupational status, whereas in interpersonal situations deference is paid on the basis of age or sex. The way deference is paid usually takes the form of an outward display of a specific mode of behavior by people occupying a lower status. This mode of behavior can be defined as non-professional in an American setting.[9]

The trait of individualism portrayed by the Indian immigrants in the American society is 'object oriented' individualism. Here interviewees strive toward professional growth, level of income, a specific lifestyle and so forth. The value is also displayed in their belief that individuals alone are responsible for their success and failure. The value has spilled over in their social life as well. Thus the interviewees agree that they have become very self-centered in the American society thinking only about their own family. Indian immigrant non-familial interpersonal relations, instead of being based on the Indian ethos of friendship, have become very status competitive and formal.

Moreover, the Indian immigrants have become very egalitarian within the American society. Thus, when asked to describe their relations with their bosses and colleagues, the majority of the Indian immigrants say it is 'one among equals' with their colleagues and 'first among equals' with their bosses. The male interviewees state that one of the reasons they may not go back to India and work could be attributed to the 'bossism' and 'non-professional work relations' that pervade the job environment in Indian society. The interviewees feel that by working in an American environment, they have lost the ability and the desire to 'boss around' or to be bossed by other people. In fact, one male interviewee, who went back to India to settle after spending six to seven years in America, returned after one year. One major reason he returned to America centered on the bossism he experienced in his work situation. This male interviewee held a very high management position in a reputable Indian company but felt like a misfit in the work environment. He reveals that his subordinates gave him a hard time since he could not openly boss them around, and his superiors gave him trouble since he would not be bossed by them. The interviewees in this study say that they have become used to the 'professional work relations' which pervade interpersonal relations in the place of work in the American society. The egalitarian orientation exhibited by the interviewees has also spilled over into their interpersonal relations within the family. Thus these males and females are more egalitarian in their attitudes toward their children and spouses than their counterparts in the Indian society.[10]

The traits portrayed by the professional women interviewees can be described as object oriented individualism whereby they compete against their own high standard of excellence and strive toward professional growth. These women are also very self-driven and believe that if they have to sit at home, they will be very frustrated and as a result will be very 'bad mothers'.

One point worth noting is that while comparing the job environment in America and in India, the female interviewees said that while their jobs are more challenging in America with a much wider scope of professional growth, they never experienced any bossism in their work place in India. However, they had very limited job experience in the Indian society, since they immigrated to America very shortly after their graduation. Yet, their point is well taken, considering the fact that whatever job experience they had in the Indian society, most likely they had it in a sex segregated environment.

The female professionals are more egalitarian in their relations with their husbands than the full-time housewives. One female professional says that she sees herself more as a 'partner' to her husband than as a wife. It can be conceptualized that, in a society, where the women are socialized to be only a 'wife' and 'mother', the professional women went for their professional roles because they were very self-driven. Yet their object oriented individualism and egalitarian orientations are reinforced by their job experiences in the American society.

The object oriented individualism, defined by Gans, has some basic similarities with the 'craftsman' qualities defined by McCoby (1976: 52). It can be safely assumed that the realization of "gamesman" qualities in American society, such as interpersonal skills to "motivate and stimulate others to work for you" (1976: 101) requires knowledge and mastery of the American code of behavior, especially if the 'others' are Americans. Such codes of behavior are virtually impossible to master by people who had their primary socialization in a different culture. Thus even the Indian immigrants have "gamesman" like traits, these traits are culturally irrelevant in the American society. It can be conjectured then that the 'craftsman' qualities that the Indian immigrants portray through their occupations, are at least, in some cases, the products of the occupational roles they are called upon to play in the American society. In other cases, however, it is these craftsman qualities which attracted the interviewees to the jobs demanding such qualities.[11]

The traits making for a craftsman, and the jobs which are based on such traits, have fitted in perfectly with the ethnic lifestyles of the Indian immigrants; a lifestyle which views occupation as one of the means in realizing one's professional skills but does not involve one total lifestyle. Thus being a craftsman has helped both males and females to maintain the desired distance between home and work.

SUMMARY AND CONCLUSION

The work life constitutes the public arena for the Indian immigrants. In order to function in this arena and be successful, the immigrant had to assimilate some of the values of the larger society. Thus we find the Indian immigrants are individualistic and believe that individuals are solely responsible for their success or failure in the work world. They also believe in materialistic productivity and problem solving orientations. The Indian immigrants, like the American middle-class show object oriented individualism. This orientation has helped them to assimilate in the work world but at the same time has led them to passive acceptance of their position on the occupational ladder. Believing as they do in individual responsibility for occupational success or failure, they blame themselves for their deficiency in communicative skills and indirectly, their ethnic background that accounts for this lack of verbal skills.

Assimilation of Indian immigrants in the work world, however, has not meant assimilation in the larger society as such. Although some work values have spilled over into their social lives, the Indian immigrants consciously separate their work place from their families. In fact, work-life forms one aspect of the lives of the Indian immigrants. They have other centers of life such as their families and communities which are equally important to them.

Dubin, while differentiating between social and organizational experiences remarks that "not only is the workplace relatively unimportant as a place of preferred human relationships but it cannot evoke significant sentiments and emotions in its occupants." (1956: 136)

Thus general social experience of emotional importance will not take place in the work place. One the other hand, Dubin reports that the workers "identified their workplace as the locale of their preferred relationships with the purely technical aspects of their environment." (1956: 138) Thus

> Industrial man seems to perceive his life history as having its center outside of work for his intimate human relationships and for his feelings of enjoyment, happiness and worth. On the other hand, for his experience with the technological aspects of his life space and for his participation in formal organizations, he clearly recognizes the primacy of the work place. In short, he has a well developed sense of attachment to his work and workplace without a corresponding sense of total commitment. (Dubin, 1956: 140)

The Indian immigrants feel that they cannot develop informal primary relationships in their workplace because any intense emotional experience on their part has to be mediated through their ethnic culture. Yet, they feel that their workplace provides them the important opportunity for organizational experience. Thus, as far as the Indian immigrants are concerned, their family as an ethnic enclave, acts as the locale for their preferred intimate human relationships.

The craftsman roles played by the Indian immigrants in their place of work help them to keep the distance between home and work. Their object oriented individualism and the 'craftsman' roles played in their job situations make them 'achievement oriented' but at the same time maintain ascriptive values within their families.[12] Thus, the roles they play in their occupational world have helped them to assimilate and not to assimilate at the same time. It has helped them to assimilate into their world of occupations but at the same time has served them to insulate their ethnic lifestyles from the stigma of the American society.

CHAPTER TEN

SUMMARY AND CONCLUSION

The ethnic patterns invoked by an ethnic group should always be related to the larger social matrix in which they are embedded (Steinberg, 1981: 138). Steinberg (1981) defines ethnicity as involving ways of thinking, feeling and acting which constitute the essence of culture. However, culture is an integral part of the larger social process. The larger social structure or the "setting" determines the overall structure of ethnic group relations, the relative political, economic and social status of these groups, and the distribution of occupation, education, income and wealth among the ethnic group members. The larger social structure or the "setting" provides the overall framework of social context defining the more microscopic "situations" in which the immigrants find themselves. Setting refers to the structural aspects of ethnicity while situation refers to the behavioral choices open to the immigrants based on their understanding of their personal circumstances. The latter encompasses the cognitive aspect of ethnicity. It refers to the perception of identity needs on the part of the

SUMMARY AND CONCLUSION

immigrants and the selection of the cultural features deemed significant by the immigrants to satisfy their identity needs. The nature of ethnicity of the Indian immigrants should be seen in the light of the dialectic between the structural and cognitive factors or between setting and situation.

The influx of the Indian immigrants to America occurred at a time when the opportunity structures existing within the American society could absorb immigrant skills and professional experiences. One of the stipulations of the 1965 Immigration Act was that only persons with professional skills needed in the American society could immigrate from the Indian subcontinent. The requirements laid down in the Immigration Act thus resulted in the immigration of upper middle-class professionals who came to America to achieve professional and intellectual growth, to enjoy better economic opportunities, to see the world or to avoid job problems in India. The opportunity structures existing within the American society made it possible for the Indian immigrants to attain middle-class status. Their training in high demand fields accorded them middle-class professional jobs.

The socio economic forces existing within the American society, thus have determined the class status of the Indian immigrants. They have also determined the social status of the Indian immigrants. The Indian immigrants are economically well off as a result of the existence of the favorable job market in the American society. But middle class economic status has not given them middle-class social status. The Indian immigrants lack the prestige of birth or position of political authority, two of the most important criteria specified by Weber to determine the social status of an individual. Thus, the Indian immigrants experience status inconsistency. They have been denied social equality and thus are structurally isolated. Structural isolation has turned the immigrants toward their ethnic group for preferred individual and institutional affiliations and for primary group relations. Ethnicity remains an important basis of their group identification. Thus the economic success of the Indian immigrants is accompanied by the stronger ethnic identification.

The social structure or the "setting" determines how the immigrants appraise the behavioral choices open to them and the different courses of action actually pursued by the actors. The course of action actually pursued by the Indian immigrants to define their identity is mostly cultural. The ethnicity of the Indian immigrants is mainly based on the cultural features chosen by them to define their identity. The Indian immigrants are quite satisfied with the economic status they occupy in the American society. They feel that

SUMMARY AND CONCLUSION

their professional success within the American society is more than what they expected to achieve although they feel that they are subject to covert discrimination. On the whole the Indian immigrants are satisfied with their economic success within the American society. They do not see the need for any concerted action as a political interest group to improve their economic status. They also feel that such concerted action would be a futile venture.

The identity needs of the Indian immigrants, thus take the form of reaffirmation of their cultural heritage. The ethnicity of the Indian immigrants is mainly cultural in nature. As members of the cultural ethnic group, the Indian immigrants share a common set of values, experiences, behavioral and linguistic traits which differ significantly from those of the members of other ethnic groups. Bank and Gay note that members of a cultural ethnic group pass on the symbols, language and cultural heritage to the next generation. The individual's ethnic and cultural heritage become a source of pride and group identification (1978: 245).

The cultural features taken into account by the Indian immigrants are dictated by their identity needs which encompass their need for group identification. The cultural features taken into account by the Indian immigrants are drawn from the repertoire of their home-based culture. Thus the chapters on Cultural Selectivity, Indian Immigrant Family and Indian Immigrant Women show that there is a definite orientation on the part of the Indian immigrants toward the Indian values of holism, and family centrism as opposed to individualism.

The value of family centrism is evident in the Indian immigrants' orientations toward their marriage and families, toward their extended families and in their child socialization practices. The Indian immigrants' commitment to Indian cultural values is expressed in viewing marriage as a life-long alliance, in traditional role expectations for the wives, in the maintenance of natal language as the medium of communication with the family members and in ethnic food habit. The maintenance of the traditional commitment of marriage has helped the Indian immigrant couples to cope with marital stress in their family structures, caused by the changes brought about by their immigration to America.

With regard to parent-child relationships, the Indian immigrants emphasize ascriptive values like respect toward parents and elders, loyalty toward immediate kin, interfamilial sociability and primary relations structured along kinship lines. The Indian immigrant women become the conservators of ethnic values within the Indian immigrant families. The value of family centrism has saved the Indian

SUMMARY AND CONCLUSION

immigrant marriages although the seclusion of the Indian immigrant family as an ethnic enclave has caused severe discontinuities in the lives of the Indian immigrant women. The seclusion has prevented the participation of the Indian immigrant women in the American society. They have become very private oriented and, therefore, they blame themselves for their self-alienation.

The ethnic values maintained by the Indian immigrants should also be seen in the light of the needs of the Indian immigrants to maintain their socio-economic status within the American society. The identity needs of the Indian immigrants are related to their needs to maintain a middle-class economic position within the American society. As a result of their professional employment, the Indian immigrants do not have to depend on social assistance and thus expose themselves to the scrutiny of the social agencies. Middle-class status protects the Indian immigrants from the pressures of the outside society to Americanize. Thus the value orientations of the Indian immigrants also encompass the values perceived by them as necessary to uphold their class position in the American society.

The cultural features selected by the Indian immigrants are conditioned by their class position in the American society. The Indian immigrants came from an upper middle-class background in India where reverence for learning and achievement are given priority (Singh, 1973: 106). But in the American society these values are given existential significance by their social class circumstances (Steinberg, 1981: 138). The class position of the Indian immigrants makes it possible for them to maintain a lifestyle which can help them to pursue these values. Their professional job environment also supports a world view which upholds academic training and competitiveness. Their professional position also helps them to see the relation between professional success, academic training and achievement orientations. Thus the ethnicity of the Indian immigrants should be seen in the light of the interaction between their ethnicity and class factors. As an "eth-class" (Gordon, 1964: 52) the members share professional, behavioral similarities with members of the professional middle class and a sense of peoplehood with members of their own ethnic group. Their sense of peoplehood is based on sharing a common identity, a common ancestral origin and a common set of values and experiences.

The Indian immigrants believe that certain value orientations are required to survive in the American society. They feel that these basic orientations on their part have already ensured their relative success in the American society, and they want to maintain these

SUMMARY AND CONCLUSION

orientations. They also want to inculcate these value orientations in their child-socialization practices. These value orientations, according to the Indian immigrants include the predominantly American values of competitiveness, achievement orientations, egalitarianism and objective individualism.

The conflict between the basic Indian values of holism and ascription and the basic American values of individualism, competitiveness, and achievement orientation is resolved by the Indian immigrants by dichotomizing between the family and community on the one hand and the outside society on the other. The Indian immigrants show orientations to Indian values within their families and orientations to American values in their occupational lives.

The Indian immigrants report competitiveness and achievement orientations in the spheres of their occupational lives. They depict cosmopolitan orientations through their commitment to their role skills rather than to their employing organizations. They are very ambitious and feel that through hard work and competitiveness they can reach the top. The Indian immigrants are also very individualistic and feel that individuals are wholly responsible for their own successes and failures. Their individualistic orientations have also led them to blame themselves for their perceived lack of verbal skills, skills they feel are absolutely necessary to be successful in the American society. The secondary socialization of the Indian immigrants in their places of work has also made them very egalitarian. The Indian immigrants contend that one of the basic obstacles in the way of their going back to India is the hierarchical practice pervading the work relations in the Indian job environment. The interviewees report that in the American society their relations with their bosses are very professional and egalitarian.

The individualism practiced by the Indian immigrants in their places of work is mainly object-oriented individualism whereby they compete against their own standard of excellence and not against other individuals. The object-oriented individualism on the part of the immigrants is part of an overall "craftsman" orientation whereby they are motivated by the challenge of work itself. Craftsman orientations (McCoby 1976: 52) make the Indian immigrants work oriented and family oriented at the same time. The craftsman qualities on the part of the Indian immigrants help them to maintain the dichotomy between family and work. These orientations have helped them to practice the Indian values of holism within their ethnic enclaves of family and community and to practice the American values of individualism, competitiveness within their job environment.

Ethnicity of the Indian immigrant is thus situational in

SUMMARY AND CONCLUSION

nature (Bank and Gay, 1978: 246). It surfaces and assumes a position of preeminence in specific spheres of social relationships in the lives of the Indian immigrants. The identity needs of the Indian immigrants determine the activities they chose to accentuate their ethnicity. In the case of the Indian immigrants, the need takes the form of reaffirmation of their cultural features within their families and communities. Thus, the ethnic values of the Indian immigrants surface and assume a position of prominence within their families and communities.

The identity needs of the Indian immigrant also take into account specific American values. The specific Indian and American values adopted by the Indian immigrants help them to maintain their ethnic identity within their ethnic enclaves and at the same time practice selected American values which would help them be successful in the American society. Thus the cultural features taken into account by the Indian immigrants are those which are regarded as significant by them to maintain their ethnic boundaries. These features are the means by which the Indian immigrants dichotomize between the outsider and the insider. They are the basis of the activities carried on by the immigrant organizations to reaffirm their ethnic identity. These specific cultural features are circumscribed by the social setting which determines the broader contours of ethnic group relations and the distribution of resources among these groups.

The class position of the Indian immigrants helps them to maintain a balance between their group cohesiveness and high achievement in the society. Their middle-class position ensures the survival of their families and communities as ethnic enclaves. Attainment of middle-class position in the American society has attenuated their preoccupation with class issues. The Indian immigrants are either satisfied with their economic class position or have given up the hope of further improving their economic status within the American society. Their structural isolation on the other hand has brought the cultural issues to the forefront. Thus the ethnicity of the Indian immigrants has taken the form of cultural affirmation of their ethnic heritage.

The cultural selectivity on the part of the Indian immigrants is thus meant to ensure their group cohesiveness and their survival in the American society. Seen in this perspective, ethnicity may be one of the ways of becoming American on the part of the Indian immigrants. As they are becoming more ethnic, they are becoming more American. Their ethnicity thus might enrich the American brew by retaining its own essence.

As for the future, the question of whether or not Indian

ethnicity debilitates or invigorates would depend upon how effective Indian ethnic enclaves are in encompassing the first generation of native-born Americans of Indian parentage under its wings. But then this question has to be answered by future researchers.

NOTES

CHAPTER THREE NOTES

1. A detailed interview schedule is given at the back.

2. The area in which interviewees took place was unique in the sense that it has been mostly inhabited by professional or semi-professional Indian immigrants. Big Cities like New York and Chigago are most likely included non-professionals within its Indian immigrant population.

3. The secondary socialization of the interviewees in the educational institutions in India provided a unique blend of traditional values and the secular values of individualism, liberalism and achievement orientations. Like the persistence of traditional values in the Indian lifestyle in general, the modern educational system in India, instead of supplanting the traditional Hindu system in India has tended to reiterate the difference between categorical and instrumental values so that the individuals exposed to the modern secular values still cherish faith in the Hindu principles of hierarchy, holism, and continuity in their social lives. But 'modernization' has created a subculture of students in India which, though not fully modern, certains elements of transition from tradition to modernity.

4. Marriages in contemporary India are still in the majority of the cases arranged by the parents (see Gupta (1974), Ramu (1977) Van Der Veen (1972)). The parents of successful sons usually look for brides for their sons from well-to-do families which would give them access to prestige, status, and power and are usually successful in establishing marriage alliances with families which are placed higher in the social ladder. Given the tight job market in India, the supply of eligible bachelors in the Indian marriage market is usually less than the demand of them.

CHAPTER FOUR NOTES

1. Data collected by Ross (1961) and Ramu (1977) show that Indian parents have very high expectations for their children, particularly for their son's accomplishments.

2. The interviewees said that their children are very much involved in different kinds of activities such as soccer league, football, music class, girl scouts, and boy scouts. They do not want to disrupt their lives.

3. The researcher shares this view with Jan Joseph DeAmicis, It Happens: American Migration to Australia, Dissertation Abstract, University of Massachusetts, 1977.

4. See Kitano (1976) for the rate of Japanese intermarriage and Lyman (1976) for the rate of Chinese intermarriage.

CHAPTER FIVE NOTES

1. By family the Indian immigrants meant the family of procreation. Although some form of obligation is also felt to the family of orientation.

2. See Maxine Fisher, "Indian Ethnic Identity: The Role of Associations in the New York Indian Population" in New Ethnics, ed. by P. Saran and E. Eames, 1980.

CHAPTER SIX NOTES

1. Ramu (1977: 35) reports that in the modern society there are many opportunities for boys and girls of marriageable age to come in contact with each other. But rarely do contacts like that go through the cycle of dating, courtship and engagement. Arranged marriages are still the rule. Thus 63% of his respondents said that their parents

chose their mates, 23% said that intimate kin chose their mates and only 8.5% said that they made the final decision about their marriage partners.

2. The average age difference between Indian couples ranges from five to ten years. The husbands are expected to be more knowledgeable and experienced.

3. The significant kin is mostly the blood relatives to whom help, monetary and other kinds are extended. The 'dinner guests' are the distant kin and close friends who are invited as dinner guests at weddings and other ceremonies.

4. Because of the status competition. See Chapter III for status competition.

5. The idea is based on W.I. Thomas's conceptualization of 'family disorganization'.

6. See the chapter on Indian Immigrant Women (Chapter VII).

CHAPTER EIGHT NOTES

1. They do not have any basis for defining working mothers as unsuccessful mothers. It is just an assumption.

2. Although the full-time housewives define professional women as unsuccessful mothers, they pay some difference to them. Thus, female physicians are consulted and their advice sought for health problems; sometimes the professional women would be praised for their financial independence. Besides, all the female interviewees want their daughters to have professional careers in fields like engineering and medicine. Thus, the female interviewees use the professional women as role models, although it is not known whether they accept the fact that they do this.

NOTES

CHAPTER NINE NOTES

1.   Craftsmen are distinguished from jungle fighters who are drawn by naked power and from Gamesmen who have all the qualities of a craftsman and company men plus a compulsive drive to be a winner and be a star and also the ability to motivate and stimulate others to his work. (McCoby, 1976: 101)

2.   The female professionals say that although they believe that sexism exists in the American society, they feel that it has not affected them. It proves that for some ethnic women ethnicism is experienced as more discriminatory than sexism.

3.   Some of them say that they cannot informally socialize with their colleagues because they feel very out of place since they are not quite familiar with American etiquettes and not very familiar with the things like fishing, hiking, skiing or American football--the things which are usually discussed when they attend their office parties.

4.   The interviewee reports that he has to go out of town three or four times a month for three or four days at a time. His wife also complains about his going out of town and she does not want him to get into a higher position where he has to travel more frequently.

5.   See Chapter VII for Indian Immigrant Women.

6.   It is very hard to speculate how they are going to support their wives. But some of the husbands of the professional women are very supportive taking major responsibility for child care and house care. The husbands mostly work regular hours, the female physicians on the other hand have to work long, irregular hours.

7.   See Chapter III for status competition.

8.   Thus in an office situation a younger officer will get more respect and deference from the older employees but relations are kept official. But in social situations deference is paid on the basis of age. This does not create any problem since officers rarely socially mix with the clerks unless they are close friends or relatives. In these situations, age becomes more important.

9.   Usually involves talking in an ordering tone, rebuking
openly lower level workers, standing up when talking to the
boss or when the boss passes, not smoking in front of the
boss, etc.

10.   See Chapter V and VI for conjugal relations and
parent child relations in an Indian immigrant family.

11.   McCoby (1976: 52) reports that all the East Indians
he interviewed were 'craftsmen' from conservative
backgrounds.

12.   McCoby says that (1976: 53) the craftsmen want to
maintain home as an enclave away from work. Objective
individualism reinforces this trait.

APPENDIX

INTERVIEW SCHEDULE

I. BACKGROUND INFORMATION:

    1. How long have you been residing in the U.S.?

    2. Number of family members in the U.S.?

    3. Number of family members in India? Say something about your family, where did your parents work?

    4. Do you belong to any Indian organizations? Any American organizations?

    5. How do you spend your leisure time in general?

II. IMMIGRATION:

    1. State how did you make the decision about immigrating to America?

    2. Whose opinions were most influential in making the decision to immigrant?

    3. What were your expectations and apprehensions before immigrating? Hopes and fears? How real they seemed after coming to U.S.?

    4. Rewards and problems in general of staying in the U.S.

    5. Reasons for staying in the U.S. in general.

III. WORK AND OCCUPATION:

    1. Describe your occupational history. How do you like your present job? Are you thinking of changing your job? Why or why not?

2. How much does your work mean to you?

3. How much do you enjoy doing the things you do as an engineer/doctor/or other?

4. What other benefits do you think you get doing the things you do as an engineer/doctor/or other?

5.
   (a) How far would you like to move up in your profession? How do you think you can do that? What obstacles you feel you have to overcome in the way of doing that? Do you think that you can do that at the expense of your family? What is the best job for you?

   (Specially for wives): What kinds of ambition you have for yourself? When you see yourself in the future what do you see happening to you? What kinds of ambitions you have for your family members? Your spouse/children?

   (b) If someone is a loser in his/her profession, do you think that he is the only one to be blamed? If there is a problem in the place of your work (like discrimination, problem of promotion, problem of interpersonal relations) would you try to solve it by yourself or do you think that you would do it by collective effort? Whose help do you think that you would ask for? your co-workers'? Your Indian friends'? Your American friends'? Indian organizations'?

   (c) What is and should be the relations between you and your boss and you and your subordinates? Do you think that subordinates should be treated like equals or like subordinates?

   Whose evaluations concern you the most? Your peers' or your boss'?

6. Imagine yourself working in India and tell me how different it is working here?

7. Do your think that your occupation is having any effect on your family?

IV. FAMILY

   1. How did you get married?

APPENDIX

(a) How important is it to you to be a father/mother; husband/wife; son/daughter; brother/sister. What are the problems of playing all these roles? In what ways are they different from playing the same role in India? Is there a problem because you are staying in the U.S.? What do you do as above which are very important to you?

2. How much do you enjoy playing the roles of father/mother etc?

3. How much benefit do you think you are getting from playing the role of father/mother etc.?

4.
(a) Who makes important decisions in your home regarding money matters, buying a house, a car, children's education, taking vacation, buying groceries, furniture. (In relations with children): Who should and does actually decide what is best for your children? What are the traits you emphasize most in your child training? With whom they should associate? What career they should choose? Whom to marry? How much money they can have? What is your idea of ideal child training? Do you think that if parents are easy on their children they would be in trouble?

(b) (With wife): Do you think that husband and wife should have private spheres of their own? Should they solve their personal problems in their own way?

(With children): At what age do you think children should be expected to depend on themselves without depending on their parents? When do you think children should make decisions affecting their own life? Like spending their own money, choosing their own friends? Choosing their own career?

(c) (With spouse): Do you think that husband and wife should have equal say in family matters like how to raise children, whom to mix with, how to spend money? Do you believe in division of labor?

(With children): Do you think that in making

family decisions parents ought to consult children?

(d) What kind of ambitions do you have for your wife and children (In the case of children): What do you want your children to be when they grow up? What is the most important thing for your child to do right now? Do you like to maintain Indian tradition or culture in your lifestyle? How do you think you can do that?

5. Comparison with India? Do you think that your relations with your spouse/children is different because you are staying in the U.S.? How is it different? Is it better or is it worse? What is the problem of having and raising a family in the U.S.?

6. What is your idea of an ideal wife/husband and ideal son/daughter?

V. EXPERIENCE VIS-A-VIS THE AMERICAN SOCIETY

1. How do you think the Americans view the Indians? What kinds of ideas do they have about the Indians?

2. What are your points of contacts with the American society?

3. What is your dominant identity in the American society?

4. How do you think the American society differs from the Indian society?

5. What are good and bad parts of the American society?

6. What are the things that the Americans can borrow from the Indians?

7. What are the traits the Indians should master in order to survive in the American society?

8. What are the advantages and disadvantages of staying in the American society as an Indian?

9. What do you think about the indian immigrants residing in the American society? What kinds of relations to you have with them?

APPENDIX

10. What are the problems of the American society?
    What can you do to solve them?

11. Are you an American citizen? Why or why not?

BIBLIOGRAPHY

Bachmann, Hedwig. On the Soul of the Indian Women as Reflected in the Folklore of the Kankan. Bastore, India: Tipografia Rangel, 1942.

Bank, James A. and Geneva Gay. "Ethnicity in Contemporary American Society: Toward a Development of Typology." Ethnicity 5, (1978): 238-281.

Barth, Frederick (ed.) Ethnic Groups and Boundaries: The Social Organization of Cultural Difference. Boston: Little Brown, 1969.

Becker, Howard S. and James Cooper. "The Elements of Identification with an Occupation." American Sociological Review 31 (1956): 341-348.

Bernard, Jessie. The Female World. New York: The Free Press, 1981.

Billingsley, Andrew. "The Structure and Functions of Negro Family Life" in Bert N. Adams and Thomas Warath (eds.) Readings on the Sociology of Family. Chicago: Markham Publishing Co., 1971: 90.

Blood, Robert O. "Resolving Family Conflicts" in Ruth S. Cavan (ed.) Marriage and Family in the Modern World. New York: Thomas J. Crowell Co., 1974: 303.

Bronfenbrenner, Urie. "Socialization and Social Class Through Time and Space" in Eleanor E. MacCoby and T.N. Newcomb and E.L. Hartley (eds.) Readings in Social Psychology, N.Y.: Henry Holt & Co., 1958: 419.

Blumer, Herbert. Symbolic Interactionism. Perspective and Method. Engelwood Cliffs, N.J.: Prentice Hall, Inc., 1959.

BIBLIOGRAPHY

Coelho, G.U. "Changing Patterns of Friendship in Modern India." Paper presented at a seminar on *Cross-Cultural Studies of Friendship*, Harvard University, May 1974.

Cohen, A. (ed.) *Urban Ethnicity*. London: Tavistock, 1974.

Coser, Rose L. (ed.) *The Family*. St. Martin's Press, N.Y., 1974.

Desai, P.N. and Mehta, D. "Indians in America--The Friendship Connection." *India Times*. May 1979.

Deshen, S. "Political Ethnicity and Cultural Ethnicity in Israel During the 1960's" in A. Cohen (ed.) *Urban Ethnicity*. London: Tavistock, 1974: 282.

Dillingham, Gerald L. 1981 "The Emerging Black Middle Class: Class Consciousness or Race Consciousness." *Ethnic and Racial Studies*, 4 (1981): 435-450.

Dollard, John. *Cast and Class in a Southern Town*. New York: Doubleday & Co., Inc., 1957.

Dubin, Robert. "Industrial Workers' Worlds." *Social Problems*, 3 (1956): 131-142.

Eisenstadt, S.N. *The Absorption of Immigrants*. London: Routledge, Kagen Paul, 1954.

Epstein, Arnold. *Ethos and Identity. Three Studies in Ethnicity*. London: Tavistock Publication, 1978.

Fichter, Joseph Henry. *Sociology*. Chicago: University of Chicago Press, 1957.

Fisher, Maxine. *The Indians of New York City*. Columbia, Missouri: South Asia Books, 1980.

Gans, Herbert H. *The Urban Villagers*. Glencoe, Illinois: The Free Press, 1962.

Gouldner, Alvin W. "Cosmopolitans and Locals: Toward an Analysis of Latent Social Roles". *Administrative Science Quarterly*, 2 (1957-58): 281-306, 444-480.

Gordon, Milton M. *Assimilation in American Life*. New York: Oxford University Press, 1964.

Gupta, Giri Raj. *Marriage, Religion and Society*. New Delhi: Nikash Publishing House Pvt. Ltd., 1974.

Hartman, Heidi. "The Family as the Locus of Gender. Class and Political Struggle." *Signs*, 6 (1981): 366-394.

Hughes, Everett C. *Men and Their Work*. Glencoe, Illinois: Free Press, 1958.

Ishwaran, Karl. *Tradition and Economy in Village India*. New York: Humanities Press, 1966.

Kallen, Horace. *Democracy Versus the Melting Pot*. New York: Boni and Liveright, 1924.

Kanter, Rosabeth Moss. *Work and Family in the U.S.* New York: Russell Sage Foundation, 1977.

Kitano, Harry L. *Japanese Americans: The Evolution of a Subculture*. Engelwood Cliffs, N.J.: Prentice Hall, Inc., 1969.

Kohn, Melvin L. "Social Class and Parent-Child Relationships." *American Journal of Sociology*. 68 (1963): 471-480.

Lasch, Christopher. *Haven in a Heartless World*. New York: Basic Books Inc., 1977.

Lewis, Oscar. *Life in a North Indian Village*. Illinois: University of Illinois Press, 1968.

Lopata, Helena Z. *Occupation: Housewife*. New York: Oxford University Press, 1971.

Lyman, Stanford M. *The Asians in North America*. California: Cilo Press Ltd., 1977.

MacCoby, Michael. *The Gamesman*. New York: Simon and Schuster, 1976.

Martin, Jean. *The Ethnic Dimension*. (Boston: George Allen), 1981.

Mitchell, Geoffrey Duncan. *The Dictionary of Sociology*. Chicago: Aldine Publishing Co., 1968.

Mitchell, J.C. "Perceptions of Ethnicity and Ethnic Behavior" in Abner Cohen (ed.) *Urban Ethnicity*, London: Tavistock Publications, 1974: 7.

Moynihan, D.P. and Nathan Glazer. *Beyond the Melting Pot*. Cambridge, Mass.: Harvard University Press, 1963.

BIBLIOGRAPHY

Myrdal, Alva and Viola Klein. *Women's Two Roles*. London: Routledge Kegan Paul, 1956.

Newell, A. "Goshen: A Gaddi Village in the Himalayas" in M.N. Srinivas (ed.) *India's Village*. Bombay: Asia Publishing House, 1955: 56.

Newman, William. *American Pluralism*. New York: Harper and Row, 1973.

Nona-Glazer, Malbin. "Housework." *Signs*, 1 (1976): 905-922.

Novak, Michael. *The Rise of the Unmeltable Ethnics*. New York: Macmillan, 1971.

Oakley, Ann. *The Sociology of Housework*. New York: Pantheon, 1974.

Okamura, Jonathan. "Situational Ethnicity." *Ethnic and Racial Studies*, 4 (1981): 453-465.

Papanek, Hannah. "Purdah in Pakistan: Seclusion and Modern Occupations for Women." *Journal of Marriage and Family*, 33 (1971): 517-530.

Park, Robert. *Race and Culture*. Glencoe, Illinois: The Free Press, 1950.

Parsons, Talcott and R. Bales. Family, Socialization and Interaction Process. Glencoe, Illinois: The Free Press, 1955.

Ramu, G.N. *Family and Cast in Urban India*. New Delhi: Vikash Publishing House Pvt. Ltd., 1977.

Rose, Peter J. (1972) *Nation of Nations: The Ethnic Experience and the Racial Crisis*. New York: Random House, 1972.

Ross, Aileen. *Hindu Family in its Urban Setting*. Toronto: Toronto University Press, 1960.

Rudolph, Lloyd I. "The Modernity of Tradition: The Democratic Incarnation of Caste in India." *American Political Science Review*, Vol. LIX, No. 4 (Dec. 1965), pp. 975-989.

Ryan, Joseph A. *White Ethnics: Life in Working Class America*. Englewood Cliffs, N.J.: Prentice Hall, 1974.

Saran, P. and Edwin Eames. *The New Ethnics*. New York: Praeger Publishers, 1981.

Scanzoni, John H. *Opportunity and the Family: A Study of Conjugal Family in Relation to Economic Opportunity Structure*. New York: Free Press, 1970.

Singh, Yogandra. *Modernization of India's Tradition*. New Delhi: Thomson Press, 1973.

Smock, Audrey and Janet Zollinger (eds.) *Women: Roles and Status in Eight Countries*. New York: Wiley, 1977: 107.

Steinberg, Stephen. *The Ethnic Myth*. New York: Altheneum, 1981.

Sutton, Francis X. et al. *The American Business Creed*. Cambridge, Mass.: Harvard University Press, 1976.

Thomas, W.I. *On Social Organization and Social Personality*. ed. by Morris Janowitz. Chicago, University of Chicago Press, 1966.

Turkel, Gerald. "Privalism and Orientation Toward Political Action." Unpublished manuscript, University of Delaware, 1977.

Van Der Veen, Klaus W. *I Give Thee My Daughter*. The Netherlands: Van Gorcum, 1972.

Vidyarthi, P. *Aspects of Religion in Indian Society*. New Delhi: Meerut, 1961.

Weber, Max. *The Theory of Social and Economic Organization*. Glencoe, Illinois: The Free Press, 1947.

INDEX

Assimilation; 3-4, 6, 10-11, 18, 61-63; amalgamation theory 8-9; anglo-conformity theory 6-9; cultural pluralism 9-10, 63-65
Assimilation, Indian; 3-4, 65-66, 117, 184-186, 198; and criticism of Americans 74, 88; cultural pluralism 78-85, 87-91, 180; non-assimilation and success 51, 55, 60-62, 186-187; and values 70

Bachmann, Hedwig; cited 24
Bales, R.; see Parsons, Talcott and R. Bales
Bank, James A. and Geneva Gay; 12-13, 191, 196-197; cited 12
Barth, Frederick; 14-16, 65; cited 15
Becker, Howard S. and James Cooper; cited 163
Bernard, Jessie; cited 146
Billingsley, Andrew; cited 119
Blood, Robert O.; 103
Blumer, Herbert; cited 22-23
Boredom; 55-57
Brofenbrenner, Urie; cited 127

Caste; see Status; Hinduism
Child socialization; 118-119, 125-130, 192, 195; adult expectations 120-126, 129; changes in 126-129; and minority status 119-120; mother's importance 99, 111-112, 127, 192; punishment 127-129
Coelho, G. U.; 85, 88, 102
Competition; status 28, 84-85, 141-142, 157-158, 176, 181
Contact, with India, visits to 51, 53, 75
Cooper, James; see Becker, Howard S. and James Cooper

Desai, P. N. and D. Mehta; 85-86, 88
Dillingham, Gerald L.; 18; cited 19
Discrimination; 138-139, 151, 191; job 166-169, 203
Divorce; 104-105, 114, 116
Dollard, John; 31
Dubin, Robert; cited 185-186

Eames, Edwin; see Saran P. and Edwin Eames
Education; 35-36; within India 2-3, 35-36, 70-71, 140, 179-180, 200; levels of immigrants 34-35; parental aid 121; of women 132-133, 135, 137-139
Eisenstadt, S. N.; 7, 61
Employment; attitudes toward 163-187, 195-196; and family importance 83, 116, 153, 163, 165-166, 170-174, 185, 204; and family tension 172-174, 203; of immigrants 36, 38, 50, 52, 60; importance of 161-162; within India 181-183, 196; obstacles 166-170; professional 2-3, 35-36, 38, 50-51, 136, 153, 162-164, 170-176, 193; and values 123-124; of women 116, 135-139, 146-151, 153, 159, 162-163, 171-176, 182, 202-203; see also Discrimination; English proficiency
English proficiency; and job advancement 166-169, 195-196
Epstein, Arnold; 16
Ethnic groups; 11-23, 61-62, 188-189; and assimilation 10-11; and class factors 17-21; cultural 12-13, 20; economic 12-13, 20; political 12-13, 20

Ethnicity/cultural identity, Indian; institutions promoting 89-90, 119, 129-130, 137-138; maintenance of 1, 4-5, 58-59, 61-62, 64, 87-91, 159-160, 176-177, 187, 190-194, 197-199; and social isolation 58-59, 61, 119-120, 150-152, 159-160, 190; and values 65-66

Family, Indian; 96-104, 113, 131, 162, 164-166, 202; changes in 116-117, 126-129, 139-140, 153-160, 173-176, 203; as culture carrier 92; family centrism 72-78, 83, 87, 90, 92-93, 105, 118, 129, 150, 159, 186, 192-193; strains on 92-93, 102-104, 113-117, 139, 172-173, 192-193, 203; structure 25, 100-106, 115, 126, 139; structure of role segregation 98-101, 106-113, 115, 117, 127, 134, 149-150, 153-154; see also Child socialization; Marriage patterns, Indian; Sexual segregation; Socio-economic status; Women
Fichter, Joseph Henry; cited 8

Gans, Herbert H.; 31, 178-179; cited 179
Gay, Geneva; see Bank, James A. and Geneva Gay
Glazer, Nathan; see Moynihan, D. P. and Nathan Glazer
Gordon, Milton M.; 13, 63, 194; cited 17
Gouldner, Alvin W.; 163-164

Hinduism; within India 70; and values 66-67, 94
Hughes, Everett C.; 177

Immigration; iii, 1-3, 39-41; motivations 39-41
Immigration Act of 1965; see Immigration regulation
Immigration, Indian; 1-3, 33-38, 40-41, 189; demography of immigrants 33-37; motivations iv, 3, 41-49, 59, 75-76, 161, 189; stresses of 50; as temporary 44, 48-50, 53-54, 57, 59; of women 47-48, 135, 143, 157
Immigration regulation; Immigration Act of 1965 1-3, 30, 35, 189; McCarren-Walter Act 1-2
Isolation, social; 54-61, 81, 190, 198; and criticism of Americans 74; and Indian family 114, 116-117; of women 56-57, 150-152, 158-160, 193

Kallan, Horace; 9
Kanter, Rosabeth M.; 177; cited 170, 174-175
Karma; see Hinduism
Kitano, Harry L.; 65
Klein, Viola; see Myrdal, Alva and Viola Klein
Kohn, Melvin L.; 120-121, 123; cited 123-124

Lasch, Christopher; 92

Marriage patterns, Indian; 34, 89, 93-95, 101, 104-105, 114, 116, 132, 192, 200, 202; arrangement of 93-95, 132-133, 200-202; equality 106, 110-112, 117, 182-183; husband/wife relationships 72, 83, 96-117, 142-145, 155, 158, 182-183; hypergamy 37; see also Divorce
Martin, Jean; 9, 63-64, 131; cited 10
McCarren-walter Act; see Immigration regulation
McCoby, Michael; 164-165, 183, 196, 204; cited 183
Mehta, D.; see Desai, P. N. and D. Mehta
Mitchell, Geoffrey Duncan; 6
Mitchell, J. C.; 13-14; cited 13
Moynihan, D. P. and Nathan Glazer; 10-11, 63; cited 4, 10-11
Myrdal, Alva and Viola Klein; 146-147

INDEX

Newman, William; 8
Novak, Michael; 18; cited 9

Okamura, Jonathan; cited 16

Papanek, Hannah; 133-134; cited 134
Park, Robert; 61; cited 6
Parsons, Talcott and R. Bales; 98, 110, 118
Privacy; importance of 25-26; of women 150, 159, 193
Purdah; see Sexual segregation

Ramu, G. N.; 93-95, 99-101, 104, 142, 201; cited 97, 100
Reverse immigration, to India; 57; and job discrimination 169; problems of return 52-53, 181, 196
Rose, Peter J.; 18
Ross, Aileen; 24-25, 95-97, 99, 102, 132-133; cited 25, 94, 96, 101, 132
Rudolph, Lloyd I.; 70
Ryan, Joseph; 18

Saran, P. and Edwin Eames; cited 74, 85
Scanzoni, John H.; 174
Settlement patterns, Indian; 37-38
Sexual segregation; 89-90, 95-96, 148; conjugal 95-98, 101, 106, 113, 140; purdah 133-135
Singh, Y.; 66, 70-71, 194; cited 67
Smock, Audrey and Janet Zollinger; 133
Social structure, Indian community; 30, 85; see also Family, Indian; Social networks, Indian
Social networks, Indian; and adjustment 56; of children 201; within the community 25-26, 29, 52; and employment 171-172, 181, 185-186, 203-204; family 96-104, 113; friendships 57, 85-87, 102, 113, 141, 171-172; traditional 96, 101; of women 56-57, 140-142, 155-157, 171-172

Status; 133, 135, 189-190; class 3-4, 41, 189; and ethnicity 18-21; within India 67, 84, 143; within U.S. 84-85; of women 139-140, 142-146, 149-150
Status, socio-economic; effects on Indians 84-85, 176; and the family 174-176; importance of 124-125, 176, 193-194, 198; Indian success 3-4, 41, 51, 60-61, 125, 189-191; of origin family 37
Steinberg, Stephen; 3, 16-17, 61-63, 188, 194; cited 17
Sutton, Francis X.; cited 178

Thomas, W. I.; 39-40; cited 39

Values, American; 68; achievement 69-70; competition 68-70; egalitarianism 68, 179; Indian adoption of 77-85, 87-88, 90-91, 118, 120-126, 128, 145, 176, 179-185, 195-198, 200; Indian criticism of 71-78, 88; individualism 68-70; work 178
Values, Indian; 66, 89-93, 120, 191-193; achievement 124-125, 186, 193-194, 201; community 67-69; value conflicts 66, 68-73, 76-78, 82-83, 88, 91, 179, 195; continuity 66-69; family 72-76, 93, 186-187; hierarchy 66-68, 70, 179-180; holism 66-69, 90, 179, 192; independence 120-123, 145; moral code 72-73; self confidence 126, 128; value changes 77-85, 87-88, 90-91, 145, 153-157, 176, 181-186, 194-198; see also Family, Indian
Van Der Veen, Klaus W.; 97
Volunteer work; 57, 137-138

Weber, Max; 18-19
World view, Indian; 24; and adjustment to U.S. 51-53, 60, 80-85, 87-88, 126-130, 183, 194, 197; of Americans 71-74, 76-79, 88; and employment 177-178, 180-187, 194; of Indians 71-74, 77-80

Women; 135-139; changes 139-147, 153-159; education of 132-133; family confinement 150-152, 193; family importance 136-137, 141, 147-149, 153, 156, 159, 173-174; female world 140-142, 157, 159; identity/self worth 148-152, 156-160; roles 98-100, 106-113, 117, 127, 132, 134, 137-139, 142-159, 192; status 139-140,

Women (Continued)
142-146, 154-159; working women 153-157, 182-183, 202; see also Education; Employment; Privacy; Sexual segregation; Social isolation; Social networks, Indian; Volunteer work

Zollinger, Janet; see Smock, Audrey and Janet Zollinger

**IMMIGRANT COMMUNITIES & ETHNIC MINORITIES
IN THE UNITED STATES & CANADA:** *continued*

31. Barbara L. Reimensnyder. *Powwowing in Union County: A Study of Pennsylvania German Folk Medicine in Context.*
32. Kaoru Oguri Kendis. *A Matter of Comfort: Ethnic Maintenance and Ethnic Style Among Third-Generation Japanese Americans.*
33. Randall Jay Kendis. *An Attitude of Gratitude: The Adaptation to Aging of the Elderly Japanese in America.*
34. Wesley R. Hurt. *Manzano: A Study of Community Disorganization.*
35. Chava Weissler. *Making Judaism Meaningful: Ambivalence and Tradition in a Havurah Community.*
36. Carolyn Stickney Beck. *Our Own Vine and Fig Tree: The persistence of the Mother Bethel Family.*
37. Charles C. Muzny. *The Vietnamese in Oklahoma City: A Study of Ethnic Change.*
38. Sathi Dasgupta. *On the Trail of an Uncertain Dream: Indian Immigrant Experience in America.*
39. Deborah Padgett. *Settlers and Sojourners: A Study of Serbian Adaptation in Milwaukee, Wisconsin.*
40. Margaret S. Boone. *Capital Cubans: Refugee Adaption in Washington, D.C.*
41. George James Patterson, Jr. *The Unassimilated Greeks of Denver.*
42. Mark M. Stolarik. *Immigration and Urbanization: The Slovak Experience.*
43. Dorita Sewell. *Knowing People: A Mexican-American Community's Concept of a person.*
44. M. Ann Walko. *Rejecting the Second Generation Hypothesis: Maintaining Estonian Ethnicity in Lakewood, New Jersey.*
45. Peter D. Goldsmith. *When I Rise Cryin' Holy: Afro-American Denominationalism on the Georgia Coast.*
46. Emily Bradley Massara. *Qué Gordita!: A Study of Weight Among Women in a Puerto Rican Community.*
47. Stephen L. Cabral. *Tradition and Transformation: Portuguese Feasting in New Bedford.*
48. Usha R. Jain. *The Gujaratis of San Francisco.*
49. Aleksandras Gedemintas. *An Interesting Bit of Identity: The Dynamics of Ethnic Identity in a Lithuanian-American Community.*
50. Suzanne J. Terrel. *This Other Kind of Doctors: Traditional Medical Systems in Black Neighborhoods in Austin, Texas.*
51. Annamma Joy. *Ethnicity in Canada: Social Accomodation and Cultural Persistence Among the Sikhs and the Portuguese.*
52. Maria Andrea Miralles. *A Matter of Life and Death: Health-seeking Behavior of Guatemalan Refugees in South Florida.*
53. Greta E. Swenson. *Festivals of Sharing: Family Reunions in America.*
54. Tekle Mariam Woldemikael. *Becoming Black American: Haitians and American Institutions in Evanston, Illinois.*
55. Louis James Cononelos. *In Search of Gold Paved Streets: Greek Immigrant Labor in the Far West, 1900—1920.*
56. Terry J. Prewitt. *German-American Settlement in an Oklahoma Town: Ecologic, Ethnic and Cultural Change.*
57. Myrna Silverman. *Strategies for Social Mobility: Family, Kinship and Ethnicity within Jewish Families in Pittsburgh.*
58. Peter Vasiliadis. *Whose Are You?: Identity and Ethnicity Among the Toronto Macedonians.*
59. Iftikhar Haider Malik. *Pakistanis in Michigan: A Study of Third Culture and Acculturation.*
60. Koozma J. Tarasoff. *Spells, Splits, and Survival in a Russian Canadian Community: A Study of Russian Organizations in the Greater Vancouver Area*
61. Alice H. Reich. *The Cultural Construction of Ethnicity: Chicanos in the University.*
62. Greta Kwik. *The Indos in Southern California.*
63. Laurence Marshall Carucci, et al. *Shared Spaces: Contexts of Interaction in Chicago's Ethnic Communities.*
64. Francis W. Chapin. *Tides of Migration: A Study of Migration Decision-Making and Social Progress in São Miguel, Azores.*
65. Robert B. Klymasz. *The Ukrainian Folk Ballad in Canada. With Musical Transcriptions by Kenneth Peacock.*
66. Elaine H. Maas. *The Jews of Houston: An Ethnographic Study.*
67. James W. Kiriazis. *Children of the Colossus: The Rhodian Greek Immigrants in the United States.*